# Biblical Cryptozoology: Revealed cryptids of the Bible

# Biblical Cryptozoology: Revealed cryptids of the Bible

∞

Dale Stuckwish

Copyright © 2009 by Dale Stuckwish.

ISBN:  Hardcover    978-1-4415-2268-9
       Softcover    978-1-4415-2267-2

All rights reserved. No part of this book may be reproduced or transmitted in any form or by any means, electronic or mechanical, including photocopying, recording, or by any information storage and retrieval system, without permission in writing from the copyright owner.

This book was printed in the United States of America.

**To order additional copies of this book, contact:**
Xlibris Corporation
1-888-795-4274
www.Xlibris.com
Orders@Xlibris.com
58993

# Contents

| | | |
|---|---|---|
| Introduction | | 7 |
| Point to ponder: Living Fossil | | 9 |
| Chapter One | Behemoth: Those Terrible Lizards | 11 |
| Chapter Two | Leviathan: Denizens from the Deep | 18 |
| Chapter Three | Satyrs: Wild Men of the Woods | 31 |
| Chapter Four | Dragons: Monsters of Land, Sea, and Air | 35 |
| Chapter Five | Unicorns: Cryptids with One Horn | 42 |
| Chapter Six | Beasts : Creatures of the Night | 48 |
| Chapter Seven | Fiery Flying Serpents: Flying Reptiles | 52 |
| Timeline | | 57 |
| Add With All Diligence These Seven Outgrowths of Faith | | 59 |
| Why I Believe and Contend for the Creation Account | | 65 |
| Creation 101 | | 67 |
| The Gap Theory: Is it Scriptural? | | 75 |
| Conclusion | | 81 |
| Biblical Cryptozoology Report | | 82 |
| Glossary of Terms | | 85 |
| References | | 89 |

# Introduction

THE WORD CRYPTOZOOLOGY first appeared in print in 1959. Before that there was not a word in the English language to describe the study of unknown creatures that were hidden or elusive to man. The word Cryptozoology comes from the Greek words "kryptos" (hidden), "zoion" (animal), "logos" (study) which means "hidden animal study". The word "cryptid" was coined by John E. Wall of Manitoba, Canada in 1983. He put this word in a letter published by the International Society of Cryptozoology. Cryptids are creatures presumed extinct, hypothetical species or creatures known from anecdotal evidence or evidence insufficient to prove their existence. Cryptozoology is not considered a true science by mainstream biologists and zoologists because of the nature of the study. But there is a truth to cryptozoology that needs revealed. It is called Biblical Cryptozoology. It is God's view of who or what these creatures are and where they came from. Because He created them. The Bible says in Colossians chapter one verses sixteen and seventeen this very fact, "For by him were all things created, that are in heaven, and that are in earth, visible and invisible, whether they be thrones, or dominions, or principalities, or powers: all things were created by him, and for him: And he is before all things, and by him all things consist." It also says in the Bible in Revelation chapter four verse eleven that they were created for God's pleasure, "Thou art worthy, O Lord, to receive glory and honour and power: for thou hast created all things, and for thy pleasure they are and were created." These creatures that are listed are revealed in God's written Word. Many of the creatures that have been seen through the centuries fall into one or more of these following categories: Behemoth, Leviathan, Satyr, Dragon, Unicorn, Beast, Fiery Flying Serpent.

# Point to ponder: Living Fossil

BEFORE I DISCUSS the categories of Biblical cryptids there is a creature that has scientists scratching their heads wondering how an animal that was believed to be extinct some 65 million years ago is able to survive all these countless generations without changing or evolving into a amphibian or becoming a land vertebrate. The "Living Fossil" that I am talking about is the Coelacanth (pronounced SEE-luh-canth) which means "hollow spine" in Greek, "coelia" meaning hollow and "acanthos" meaning spine. The scientific name for this creature is "Latimeria chalumnae". It is a member of a group of fishes called Crossopterygians. They are lobe-finned fish with the pectoral and anal fins on fleshy stalks supported by bones, and the tail or caudal fin diphycercal (divided into three lobes), the middle one of which also includes a continuation of the notochord. They are related to lungfishes.

The first mounted captured specimen was a 5 foot long, 127 pound large scaled blue colored fish brought up in a net off South Africa by Captain Hendrick Goosen, of the fishing trawler NERINE, who was fishing off the east coast of South Africa, near the Chalumna River. On December 23, 1938 Goosen telephoned Marjorie Courtenay-Latimer, curator at East London's small museum northeast of Cape Town, to come look at his haul. She in turn, called Professor James Leonard Brierley Smith to look at the fish she found in Goosen's catch. He recognized it as a coelacanth, known only from fossils. Professor Smith named the fish Latimeria chalumnae in honor of Marjorie Courtenay-Latimer and the waters in which it was found. This fish became known as a "living fossil". This coelacanth is still on display in the East London Museum.

### NOW FOR THE REST OF THE STORY!

First point to ponder, evolutionary scientists say the coelacanth first appeared in the fossil record in the Middle Devonian, about 410 million years ago and became extinct about 65 million years ago with the so called dismise of the dinosaurs. But the fossils they found of it and the specimens they caught of it have the same skeletal characterization. In layman's terms they are the same. Surely after millions upon millions of years there should of been a change. Could it be that they only been around for thousands of years. Could it be the evidence from the coelacanth is good evidence for creation. In other words, the coelacanth has reproduced after its kind just like the Bible's book of Genesis said fishes would. Genesis chapter one verses twenty through twenty-three gives us this account.

Second point to ponder, we can give God the glory for creating such a creature that survived the worldwide Noahic flood and we are able to see this creature today.

My hope in writing this book is to glorify my Lord and Saviour Jesus Christ and give Him the thanks for creating these creatures that are found in the Bible.

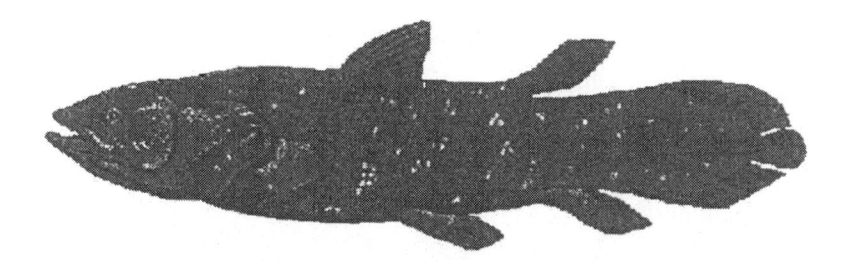

Coelacanth
Latimeria chalumnae

# "Behemoth: Those Terrible Lizards"

"**B**EHOLD NOW BEHEMOTH, which I made with thee; he eateth grass as an ox. Lo now, his strength is in his loins, and his force is in the navel of his belly. He moveth his tail like a cedar: the sinews of his stones are wrapped together. His bones are as strong pieces of brass; his bones are like bars of iron. He is the chief of the ways of God: he that made him can make his sword to approach unto him. Surely the mountains bring him forth food, where all the beasts of the field play.

"He lieth under the shady trees, in the covert of the reeds, and fens. The shady trees cover him with their shadow; the willows of the brook compass him about. Behold, he drinketh up a river, and hasteth not: he trusteth that he can draw up Jordan into his mouth. He taketh it with his eyes: his nose pierceth through snares." (Job 40:15-24)

## INTRODUCTION

Job seen something enormous in a river near where he lived at in the land of Uz (Job 1:1). Job's description of this beast that he saw had to be huge. Because he described the tail of the behemoth as being huge. He said that the beast "moveth his tail like a cedar" (Job 40:17a). Plus he said that this beast "drinketh up a river" (Job 40:23a). The creature Job saw God called it "behemoth". The word "behemoth" is only mentioned one time in our Bible (King James Version). Many commentaries say that behemoth is said to be a hippopotamus. Eventhough the hippopotamus lives near and in rivers this is not what Job probably saw. The hippopotamus has only a short tail about 22 inches long. That would quickly eliminate this animal because the hippopotamus definately does not have a tail like a cedar.

Hippopotamus

I believe Job saw something so awesome that God wanted to show Job how great He was as Creator and wanted Job to observe some of these magnificent creatures that He created on the sixth day of Creation.

God said to Job, "Behold now behemoth, which I made with thee; he eateth grass as an ox." (Job 40:15)

God said in Genesis 1:24-31 that He created land animals and man on the sixth day of Creation.

I believe this creature that Job seen was one type of land animal that God created that we call "DINOSAURS". The word "DINOSAUR" is definitely not in our Bible. It is a Greek word meaning "Terrible Lizard".

For Job to see this creature I believe this type of land animal had to be on Noah's Ark. Because in order for him to see it this dinosaur's parents or maybe this dinosaur itself along with its mate had to be on the Ark in order for it to survive the world-wide flood. Genesis 7:21-23 says, "And all flesh died that moved upon the earth, both of fowl, and of cattle, and of beast, and of every creeping thing that creepeth upon the earth, and every man: All in whose nostrils was the breath of life, of all that was in the dry land, died. And every living substance was destroyed which was upon the face of the ground, both man, and cattle, and the creeping things, and the fowl of the heaven; and they were destroyed from the earth: and Noah only remained alive, and they that were with him in the ark."

## "BEHOLD NOW BEHEMOTH" – DINOSAUR

Man has been awestruck about dinosaurs because of their appearance ever since the sixth day of Creation when man was created by God. Adam who named all the land animals (Genesis 2:19) had to be awestruck when he saw these magnificent creatures for the first time.

I was awestruck when I was a child and saw these enormous fossil skeletons of dinosaurs (Diplodocus*, Tyrannosurus Rex, Stegosaurus) when I went on a field trip with the school to the Carnegie Museum of Natural History in Pittsburgh, Pennsylvania for the first time. Just think how they would of looked with flesh on those bones and were moving around.

Diplodocus

Diplodocus was the longest member of a group of dinosaurs called sauropods. The sauropods were giant plant eating dinosaurs. They were the largest land animals ever to have lived. The Blue Whale a marine mammal is the largest animal that exists now. Diplodocus had a long flexible neck, a relatively short body, and a long whip like tail. Its long head, small for an animal so large, held a relatively small brain. It had weak pencil-like teeth used for plucking soft leaves or sniping off water plants. These teeth were only in the front of the jaws. Diplodocus must have swallowed its food whole. Along with the food it may have taken in stones and stored them in a muscular organ similar to a bird's gizzard. The stones helped to grind up the food.

The name "Diplodocus" means "double-beamed" in Greek. It refers to the forked spines on the dinosaur's vertebrae.

To get back to what Job saw "Behold now behemoth". I believe this behemoth could of been something similiar to the Diplodocus. It most definitely has a tail that "moveth like a cedar" and he most definitely could look like he could "drinketh up a river".

The Diplodocus that is in the Carnegie museum is about 90 feet long. The Blue Whale which is the largest animal (marine mammal) on the Earth today grows to about the same size.

*The blue whale is the largest mammal ever to have lived on earth. Ironically, it feeds on some of the smallest ocean life – plankton.*

The dinosaur that Job saw was a plant-eating type dinosaur. Because God told him that this "behemoth" which He saw was created the same time He created man and that it ate grass like an ox. "Behold now behemoth, which I made with thee; he eateth grass as an ox." (Job 40:15)

God also said to Job that the behemoth's "bones are as strong pieces of brass; his bones are like bars of iron." (Job 40:17)

*Comparison of the bones of a Hippopotamus and a Dinosaur.*

God told Job that this behemoth (dinosaur) was "Chief of the ways of God" and that where he lived was mostly in and near swamps and rivers. "He lieth under the shady trees, in the covert of the reeds and fens. The shady trees cover him with there shadow; the willows of the brook compass him about." (Job 40:21-22)

What a magnificent and awesome creature Job had the opportunity to see in the flesh. I believe there might be a few of these behemoths (dinosaurs) left. There has been reported sightings of dinosaurs even up to this present day. There has been articles written about these sightings in newspapers, magazines and other periodicals. There has been reports from explorers and natives in Africa of dinosaur-like creatures. These reports usually been confined to out-of-the-way places such as lakes in middle of the Congo jungles. The natives in this region call this creature "mokele-mbembe".

# BEHOLD NOW BEHEMOTH

## MOKELE-MBEMBE
## (DINOSAUR)

On the basis of two investigatory expeditions, made in 1980 and 1981, Dr. Roy P. Mackal, a research biologist at the University of Chicago, is convinced of the existence of a legendary monster in the swampy Ubangi-Congo basin of central Africa. Known as mokele-mbembe and described by the Congo pygmies as half-elephant, half-dragon, and much more fearsome than a crocodile, the creature has been dodging hunter-explorers since the start of the 20th century – although reports of something weird in central African rivers and swamps go back to the 1800's.

In 1980 Roy Mackal and James H. Powell, Jr., a crocodile specialist, went deep into the heart of the wild Likouala region to track the tales to their source and try to identify the beast. They arrived at the remote outpost of Impfondo early in February, and although they were appalled by the trackless swamps and jungles that lay ahead, they were heartened to hear locally that the mokele-mbembe was often spoken of as a well-known phenomenon if unfamiliar beast.

One of the older eyewitness reports was given by one Firman Mosomele, who said that about 45 years earlier, when he was a 14-year-old, he had seen the creature while paddling his canoe around a bend on the Likouala aux Herbes River near the town of Epéna. He waited only long enough to see a reddish-brown snakelike head and neck about six to eight feet long before he paddled briskly away, but the image was burned on his brain. When shown a book of animal pictures, Mosomele picked a sauropod (or dinosaur) as the creature he had seen.

The next report, by a woman from Epéna, confirmed that such a creature was indeed a habitué of that area. Two of the beasts, she said, had recently entered Lake Tele from the Bai River. One had been killed by lakesiders, then cut up and eaten in spite of a local belief that people eating its flesh would soon die.

The explorers and their porters spent most of the rest of the month "slogging" through mokele-mbembe territory, hunting the creature and colleting many more eyewitness accounts. One of the most circumstantial was given by Nicolas Mondongo, a Congolese from the village of Bandéko. During a journey on the Likouala aux Herbes between Mokengui and Bandéko he saw a mokele-mbembe "making the water run backwards as it rose out of the river."

The water at that point was only three to six feet deep, and virtually the whole animal was visible. Mondongo said he saw its back, neck, head, part of a long tail, and short legs. The head was topped with something like a cockscomb. As nearly as he could judge, the length of the creature was 32 feet, about 6 to 10 feet of which were head and neck.

Convinced by such reports that "although rare, the *mokele mbembes* do exist and that they correspond to no other living forms known to science," Dr. Mackal returned to Africa in 1981 on a six-week expedition with a group of French, American, and Congolese scientists. Their foray was highlighted by the discovery of "huge footprints and a wide swath of bent and flattened vegetation. The track led into a river." In size the footprints compared with those of an elephant, according to Dr. Mackal, but the flattened vegetation suggested that the trail had been made by a reptilian creature "taller and larger than any known crocodile."

Dr. Mackal, who is "more convinced now than ever" of the creature's existence, thinks that it inhabits swamps but uses the rivers to facilitate moving about. Further ventures in search of the beast are expected.

# Leviathan: Denizens from the Deep

**P**SALMS 104:26 THERE go the ships: there is that leviathan, whom thou hast made to play therein.

Job 41:1 Canst thou draw out leviathan with an hook? or his tongue with a cord which thou lettest down? 2 Canst thou put an hook into his nose? or bore his jaw through with a thorn? 3 Will he make many supplications unto thee? will he speak soft words unto thee? 4 Will he make a covenant with thee? wilt thou take him for a servant for ever? 5 Wilt thou play with him as with a bird? or wilt thou bind him for thy maidens? 6 Shall the companions make a banquet of him? shall they part him among the merchants? 7 Canst thou fill his skin with barbed irons? or his head with fish spears? 8 Lay thine hand upon him, remember the battle, do no more. 9 Behold, the hope of him is in vain: shall not one be cast down even at the sight of him? 10 None is so fierce that dare stir him up: who then is able to stand before me? 11 Who hath prevented me, that I should repay him? whatsoever is under the whole heaven is mine. 12 I will not conceal his parts, nor his power, nor his comely proportion. 13 Who can discover the face of his garment? or who can come to him with his double bridle? 14 Who can open the doors of his face? his teeth are terrible round about. 15 His scales are his pride, shut up together as with a close seal. 16 One is so near to another, that no air can come between them. 17 They are joined one to another, they stick together, that they cannot be sundered. 18 By his neesings a light doth shine, and his eyes are like the eyelids of the morning. 19 Out of his mouth go burning lamps, and sparks of fire leap out. 20 Out of his nostrils goeth smoke, as out of a seething pot or caldron. 21 His breath kindleth coals, and a flame goeth out of his mouth. 22 In his neck remaineth strength, and sorrow is turned into joy before him. 23 The flakes of his flesh are joined together: they are firm in themselves; they cannot be moved. 24 His heart is as firm as a stone; yea, as hard as a piece of the nether millstone. 25 When he raiseth up himself, the mighty are afraid: by reason of breakings they purify themselves. 26 The sword of him that layeth at him cannot hold: the spear, the dart, nor the habergeon. 27 He esteemeth iron as straw, and brass as rotten wood. 28 The arrow cannot make him flee: slingstones are turned with him into stubble. 29 Darts are counted as stubble: he laugheth at the shaking of a spear. 30 Sharp stones are under him: he spreadeth sharp pointed things upon the mire. 31 He maketh the deep to boil like a pot: he maketh the sea like a pot of ointment. 32 He maketh a path of shine after him; one would think the deep to be hoary. 33 Upon earth there is not his like, who is made without fear. 34 He beholdeth all high things: he is a king over all the children of pride.

    The "leviathan" the Bible talks about is described in detail in Job chapter forty-one verses one through thirty-four. This creature that God created is stronger than any known animal of the sea. Leviathan is a creature of the water (rivers, lakes, oceans) while his contempary was behemoth (mostly land dwelling). The leviathan were still being seen during the time of King David. Psalm 104 says they played where the ships go to and fro. The Mediterranean Sea is probably the place they were probably being seen.

    The leviathan according to Scripture was large with strong jaws and great teeth. It was a fast swimming creature and had tough skin to protect it from being captured. Some sea creatures that fit the description are the ancient plesiosaurs, mosasaurs, and pliosaurs. These creatures have been seen recently in lakes and oceans around our world. The most famous creature that comes to mind that has been seen by countless witnesses is the Loch Ness Monster or Nessie for short. It has been seen in Scotland, the northern part of England. Other famous creatures that are believed to inhabit North American lakes are Champ of Lake Champlain, USA, Ogopogo of Lake Okanagan, Canada and Manipogo of Lake Manitoba, Canada. There is also some famous leviathans that inhabit the coastal waters of North America such as Caddy (Cadborosaurus willsi) of the Pacific coast and Chessie in the Chesapeake bay off the Atlantic coast are but a few of these creatures.

There has been fossils found of Kronosaurus, Elasmosaurus, Basilosaurus or Zeuglodon, and Tanystropheus that fit leviathan to a tee. These creatures had backbones that were very flexible. They could probably swim with a snake-like motion.

## Kronosaurus

Pronounced KROH-nó-SORE-us which means "lizard of Kronos" It was among the largest plisosaurs with a total length of 43 feet. It had a skull of over 10 feet long and teeth that measured 10 inches. He was truly a jaws of the seas. He had a thick head, short neck and a stocky body. He could dive very deeply, but because he was a reptile, he needed to come to the surface for air. His diet consisted of Mollusks, fish, and other marine reptiles.

Kronosaurus gets its name from the leader of the Greek Titans, Kronos. He was a greek god, who ate his own children to jealously guard his power.

A complete fossil skeleton of the species Kronosaurus queenslandicus is currently in the Queensland Museum in Australia

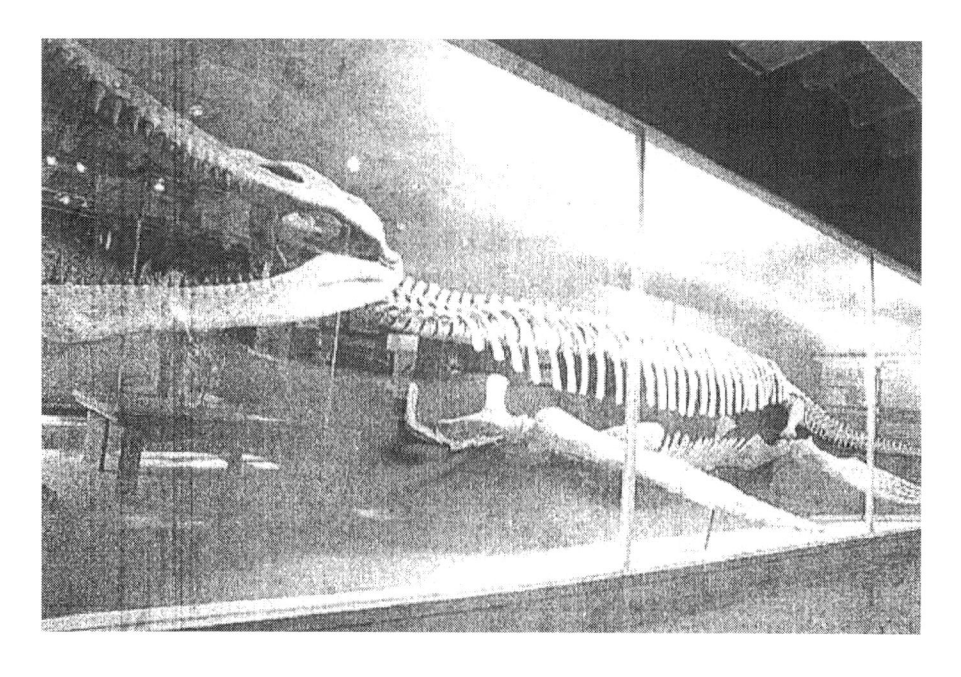

*Kronosaurus* skeleton.

# Elasmosaurus

Pronounced ee-LASS-moh-SORE-us. It was about 46 feet in length and weighed over 2.2 tons, making it the longest plesiosaur. It had a large body and four flippers for limbs. It was a slow swimmer. He could truly reach out and touch someone with that long neck. Especially fish that were faster than him. More than half of length of his body was neck, which had more than 70 vertebrae, more than any other animal. It had a relatively small head with a lot of sharp teeth. Elasmosaurus comes from the Greek meaning "thin plate" (referring to thin plates in its pelvic girdle) "lizard".

Many people believe the Elasmosaurus is not only the sea monster sailors have been seeing since ancient times, but he may also be the famous "Loch Ness Monster".

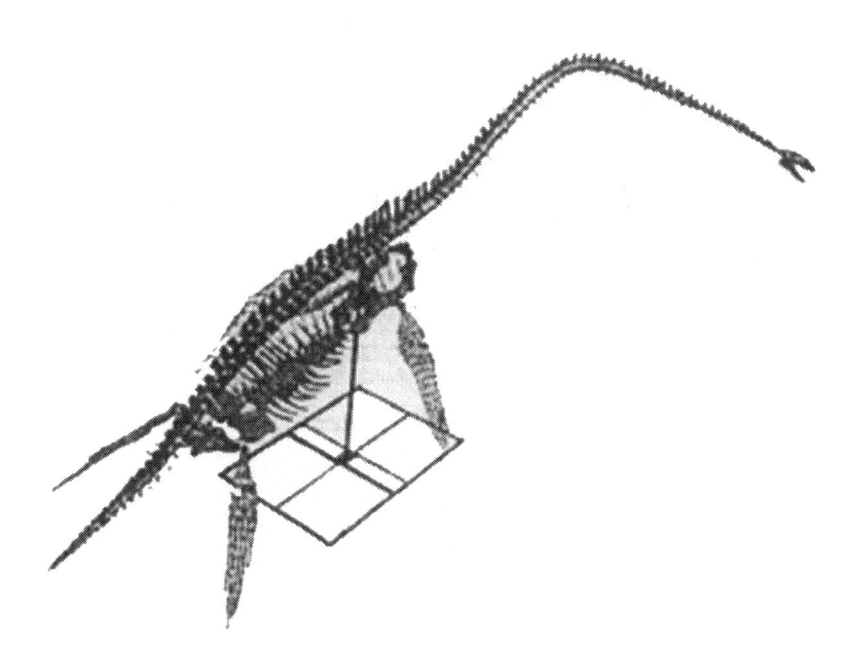

## Basilosaurus

From the Greek meaning "King Lizard" or King of the Reptiles. Its fossilized remains were first discovered in the southren United States in the state of Louisiana and was initially believed to be some sort of reptilian sea monster, hence the suffix- "saurus". There has been at least two other specimens found in Zueglodon valley in Egypt and in Pakistan. Basilosaurus averaged about 60 feet in length, and displayed an unparalleled degree of elongation compared with modern whales. Basilosaurus is the state fossil of Mississippi and Alabama.

# Tanystropheus

Pronounced TAN-eeSTROH-fee-us. This bizarre animal was not a dinosaur. But a reptile with an incredibly long neck. Three quarters of its body length was its neck and tail. Its neck was 10 feet long, which is longer than its body and tail put together. The neck had only ten vertebrae that were so long (some were over a foot long) that they first thought they were bones from a leg. Because the bones were so large, the neck was rather stiff but somewhat flexible, The neck was like a fishingrod. He walked on four legs that had webbed feet. He was not a fast swimmer and often walked along the seabed, using its long neck to get within range of prey.

Fossils of Tanystropheus have been found in Europe and the Middle East. The first Tanystopheus fossil was discovered and named by von Meyer in 1855.

## Loch Ness Monster

The Loch Ness Monster is a legendary creature claimed to inhabit Scotland's Loch Ness, the most voluminous freshwater lake in the United Kingdom.

Along with Bigfoot and the Yeti, the Loch Ness Monster is one of the best-known claims of cryptozoology. Cryptozoology is not generally accepted by the scientific community, but belief in the legend persists around the world. Local people, and later many around the world, have affectionately referred to the animal by the diminutive of Nessie (Scottish Gaelic: "Niseag").

---

Loch Ness Monster (Nessie)

The "Surgeon's photo" (1934), later revealed as a hoax

| | |
|---|---|
| Creature | |
| Name: | Loch Ness Monster (Nessie) |
| AKA: | *Nessiteras rhombopteryx*, |
| | Nessie, |
| | Niseag (Scottish Gaelic) |
| Classification | |
| Grouping: | Cryptid |
| Sub grouping: | Lake monster |
| | Data |
| First reported: | 565 (legend) |
| Last sighted: | Present day |
| Country: | Scotland |
| Region: | Loch Ness |
| Habitat: | Water |
| Status: | Unconfirmed |

---

Loch Ness

*Pictures suggest that the elusive creature sought in Loch Ness is linked to the elasmosaur, a type of plesiosaur*

## Champ

Champ or Champy is the name given to a reputed lake monster living in Lake Champlain. The creature's existence has never been authoritatively documented. While most authorities regard Champy as legend, some believe it is possible such a giant creature does live deep in the lake. The state government of Vermont has put Champ on its Endangered Species List, so that if such an animal does exist, it would be protected by law.

When people hear phrases like "sea monster" or "lake monster", they often think of mythical giant squid-like creatures or some kind of merfolk out in the middle of the ocean. Many may think of the affectionately-named "Nessie" from Loch Ness in Scotland. However, the lore of lake monsters also exists in North America. According to legend and eye witness accounts, such as monster dwells in Lake Champlain, a 125-mile-long body of fresh water that is shared by New York and Vermont and juts a few miles into Quebec, Canada.

Champ is highly revered by many in the area and has become a revenue-generating attraction. For example, the village of Port Henry, New York, has erected a giant model of Champ and holds "Champ Day" on the first Saturday of every August.

The mascot of Vermont's lone Minor League Baseball affiliate, the Vermont Expos, Champ would became even more of the star of the team when they would rename the team, due to the end of the Montreal Expos, to the Vermont Lake Monsters. Champ has been the primary attraction of the New York – Penn League affiliate since their inception.

In 1977, Sandra Mansi photographed Champ while she was having a picnic with friends. This is the best known photograph of Champ . . . it was published by Time and various other magazines. Champ has been featured on NBC TV's *Unsolved Mysteries* and Fox Network's *Sightings*, as well as on Japanese television and The Today Show. It has been the subject of books and hundreds of newspaper articles.

## Ogopogo

Okanagan Lake in British Columbia, connected to the Pacific via the Columbia River, is said to be the habitat of a huge aquatic animal popularly known as Ogopogo. Reported about 200 times since the year 1700, the creature was observed at close range by several people on July 2, 1949. Mr. Leslie L. Kerry of Kelowna, having left his wife at their house overlooking the lake, was treating the W. F. Watson family of Montreal to a boat ride when they spotted a large, snakelike form in the water. Undulating vertically the object traveled sometimes above and sometimes below the surface of the lake. The people in the boat – adults and children – saw a body about 30 feet long and perhaps a foot in diameter, with a forked tail that lashed up and down.

Mrs. Kerry saw the event from the shore and called her neighbors, Dr. and Mrs. Stanley Underhill. All rushed down to the beach and trained binoculars upon the creature, which remained in view for at least 15 minutes. Dr. Underhill described it as smooth and black and having "undulations or coils" about seven feet long. He thought there were at least two creatures because of the distance between some of the coils. Ogopogo, it would seem, is not alone.

Representatives of the media seldom have the good fortune to be present at a monster sighting, but one journalist boating on Okanagan Lake near the town of Vernon got lucky on July 17, 1959 – although not lucky enough to have a camera handy. Mr. R. H. Miller, editor of the *Vernon Advertiser*, was accompanied by his wife, their friends Mr. and Mrs. Pat Marten, and the Martens's son Murray. They were on their way home early that evening when Miller noticed a large creature following in the wake of their motor cruiser at a distance of about 250 feet. Pat Marten, who was steering, turned the boat around for a better view.

As they slowly drew closer, the Millers and Martens studied the creature through binoculars and were unable to reconcile its blunt-nosed, snakelike head with that of any animal they knew. Itself apparently none too pleased at what it saw, the creature gradually submerged and disappeared from view.

The Ogopogo, known under the Salish name of N'ha·a·itk, or Naitaka, has existed in local myth for an unknown period of time and pre-dates western settlement of the area, as do native references to the "Great-beast-in-the-lake" and the "Snake-in-the-lake" and Petroglyphs, or pictographs found near the headwaters of Powers Creek, showing a serpent-like beast, which may represent the earliest evidence of legend's existence.

Tribes in Okanagan were always wary of traveling across the lake and often carried animals that could be sacrificed in the event that the creature as sighted, and it was documented in the history of Okanagan Mission that none of the local populace were willing to fish near Squally Point, where they believed the entrance of Ogopogo's cave was located.

Ogopogo

A statue of the Ogopogo in a park in Kelowna, British Columbia

| Creature | |
|---|---|
| Name: | Ogopogo |
| AKA: | N'ha·a·itk, Naitaka |
| Classification | |
| Grouping: | Cryptid |
| Sub grouping: | Lake monster |
| Data | |
| First reported: | 1860 + prior local legend |
| Country: | Canada |
| Region: | Lake Okanagan, British Columbia |
| Habitat: | Water |
| Status: | Unconfirmed |

## Cadborosaurus willsi

"*Cadborosaurus willsi*", nicknamed "Caddy", is the name given to a sea serpent reported to be living on the Pacific Coast of North America. Its name is derived from Cadboro Bay in Victoria, British Columbia, and the Greek root word "*sauros*" meaning lizard or reptile. The animal is similar in form and behavior to various popularly named lake monsters such as "Ogopogo" of deep interior lakes of British Columbia and to the Loch Ness Monster of Scotland.

There have been more than 300 claimed sightings during the past 200 years, including San Francisco Bay, California and Deep Cove in Saanich Inlet, B. C.

*Cadborosaurus willsi* is said to resemble a serpent with vertical coils or humps in tandem behind the horse-like head and long neck, with a pair of small elevating front flippers, and a pair of large webbed hind flippers fused to form a large fan-like tail region that provides powerful forward propulsion. It has been proposed that through a process of locomotory body transformation, the long slender body can be doubled up into rigid vertical humps that effectively reduce the contact area of the snakelike body surface with the water and enable the animal to attain speeds of more than 40 km/h at the surface.

---

*Cadborosaurus willsi*

"*Cadborosaurus*" carcass,
photographed in October, 1937.

| | |
|---|---|
| Creature Name: | *Cadborosaurus willsi* |
| AKA: | Caddy |
| Classification | |
| Grouping: | Cryptid |
| Sub grouping: | Sea monster |
| Data | |
| Country: | Canada |
| Region: | Pacific Coast |
| Habitat: | Sea |
| Status: | Unconfirmed |

---

The existence of the species has been suggested by the original specimen-based description in a refereed scientific journal in which the type juvenile specimen is represented by 3 different close-up quality photographs (in the B. C. Provincial Archives in Victoria), in which at least three new-born relatively tiny precocial "baby" specimens have been independently held by at least three pairs of human captors during the past 40 years, and by more than 100 documented sightings, photographs, sonar images, and sketches of live animals made independently at predicted times and places, subsequent to the original description in 1995 and continuing to the present.

# Satyrs: Wild Men of the Woods

This image is from the film that Roger Patterson shot
on October 20, 1967, at Bluff Creek, California.

"**B**UT WILD BEASTS of the desert shall lie there; and their houses shall be full of doleful creatures; and owls shall dwell there, and satyrs shall dance there." Isaiah 13:21

"Satyrs are mentioned one time in the Bible in Isaiah 13:21, "But wild beasts of the desert shall lie there; and their houses shall be full of doleful creatures; and owls shall dwell there, and satyrs shall dance there." And "satyr" is mentioned one time in Isaiah 34:14, "The wild beasts of the desert shall also meet with the wild beasts of the island, and the satyr shall cry to his fellow; the screech owl also shall rest there, and find for herself a place to rest."

There translation from the Hebrew means faun, he goat or hairy one (shaggy). They were creatures with the legs of a goat and upper body of a monkey or human. In Greek mythology they were considered gods of the woods or mountains.

There is a connection with these creatures and creatures that are being seen today such as the Abominable Snowman or Yeti, legendary wildmen of the Himalayas. Reports of sightings have come from Nepal (where the creature is known as Yeti) and from parts of Siberia, China and other areas of Asia. Sightings have also been reported in North America, where the Abominable Snowman is called Bigfoot in the USA and Sasquatch in Canada. These creatures are said to be elusive; to be heavily built, apelike, hairy and have a distinct malodorous smell, with facial features resembling those of a human being. They have no language but communicate by grunts, cries or whistles. Some theorists believe that these reports of the Yeti and other wildmen of the woods are nothing more than modern variations of an ancient mythological theme. Some sightings have indeed been hoaxes perpetuated to make financial gain. However, it has been argued that the widespread presence of these creatures in folklore indicates that they have actually existed since ancient times and may still inhabit remote regions of the earth. Other theories on these sightings of these creatures are an unkown species of ape or creatures connected with UFO sightings or could these creatures come from a spiritual realm.

## Could satyrs be Spirit creatures?

In Greek mythology they considered them as gods. They inhabitated the woods and mountains. Through the centuries there has been sightings of these creatures by every culture. To the Greeks they looked like half man and half goat. To other cultures they appeared in a different form. They have the ability to shape-shift. God did not only create in the physical world He also created in the spiritual world. "For by him were all things created, that are in heaven, and that are in earth, visible and invisible, whether they be thrones, or dominions, or principalities, or powers all things were created by him, and for him." Colossians 1:16. These creatures can look like a UFO then change into another shape. They can levitate, walk, run, or disappear and then appear in another place.

A new element had begun to filter into the worldwide composite portrait of large upright monsters by the 1970's: a possible connection between *some* unidentified bipeds and the UFO phenomenon. A curious episode of the UFO kind occurred one night in August 1972 at Roachdale, Indiana, where a family named Rogers lived in a trailer home.

The sequence of events began when one of the Rogers saw a luminous object hovering in the sky over a nearby cornfield. On several occasions thereafter all the Rogers heard noises in the yard at night, and when one of the men went outside to investigate, he caught a glimpse of a large, heavily built creature parting the cornstalks. Once, Mrs. Rogers saw it looking in through her trailer window and observed that it stood like a man but ran on all fours.

The sightings were never very clear, for they always took place at night, but the Rogers could tell that the creature was covered with black hair – and it had an odor "like dead animals or garbage." A unique feature of the beast was that it appeared to lack substance:

> What was weird was that we could never find tracks, even when it ran over mud. It would run and jump but it was like somehow it wasn't touching anything. When it ran through weeds, you couldn't hear anything. And sometimes when you looked at it, it looked like you could see *through* it.

Yet the monster was not altogether insubstantial. Among the others who saw it were several farmers, who found dozens of mutilated – though uneaten – chickens after visits from the beast. The Burdines found dead chickens, trampled grass, and a broken fence on their property. The pigs' food bucket, the Burdines further noted, had been emptied of tomatoes and cucumbers. One night they saw the apparent culprit standing in the doorway of their chicken house. According to Junior Burdine:

This thing completely blocked out the lights inside the chickenhouse. The door is 6 x 8'. Its shoulders came up to the top of the door, up to where the neck should have been. But this thing didn't have a neck. To me it looked like an orang-utan or a gorilla. It had long hair, with kind of a brownish cast to it. Sort of rust-lookin' color. I never saw its eyes or its face. It was making a groaning racket.

The Burdine men chased and shot at the creature when it ran, but though the range was short and they were certain they had hit it, it appeared to be unhurt.

# Dragons: Monsters of Land, Sea, and Air

"Speak and say, Thus saith the Lord GOD; Behold, I am against thee, Pharoah King of Egypt, the great dragon that lieth in the midst of his rivers which hath said, My river is mine own, and I have made it for myself." Ezekiel 29:3

THE WORD "DRAGON" is mentioned 6 times in the Old Testament and 13 times in thr New Testament all in the Book of the Revelation which describes the Devil. The word "dragons" is mentioned 16 times in the Old Testament and 0 times in the New Testament. The references all describe an animal. The Hebrew word use is "tanniym" which means a marine or land monster, sea serpent, dragon, sea monster.

Dragons are believed to be mythical creatures that did not exist. But the Bible describes as real live creatures. Dragons were generally evil and destructive. Every country had them in its mythology. In Greece, dragons were slain by Hercules, Apollo, and Perseus. Beowulf killed a dragon in an Anglo-Saxon epic poem in Old English literature. The only existing manuscript of Beowulf is in the British Library. The Chinese believe the dragon is a god and use the symbol as a kingly emblem

When people think of dragons they think of fire-breathing gigantic creatures that fly. But there is actually a creature that is called a dragon. It is the Komodo dragon of Indonesia. They are giant monitor lizards that roam wild on the Komodo islands. They measure up to 10 feet and weigh up to 300 lbs. and can live 100 years.

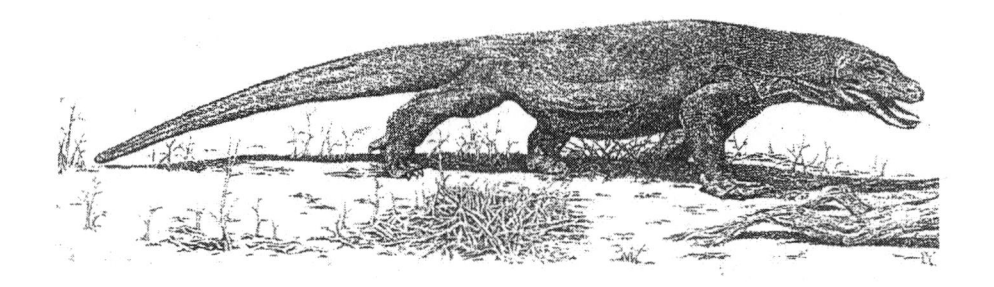

## Megalania

| | |
|---|---|
| | *Megalania* |
| | Megalania skeleton |
| | Melbourne Museum |
| | Conservation status |
| | Extinct (fossil) |
| | Scientific classification |
| Kingdom: | Animalia |
| Phylum: | Chordata |
| Class: | Sauropsida |
| Order: | Squamata |
| Suborder: | Lacertilia |
| Infraorder: | Platynota |
| Superfamily: | Varanoidea |
| Family: | Varanidae |
| Genus: | Megalania |
| Species: | M. *prisca* |
| | Binomial name |
| | *Megalania prisca* |
| | (Richard Owen, 1859) |

*Megalania* is an extinct giant monitor lizard. It was one of the megafauna that roamed southern Australia, and appears to have become extinct around 4,000 years ago. It was once thought to belong to a distinct monotypic genus and called *Megalania prisca*, (Greek Μέγασ + ἡλαίνω "giant roamer", "in reference to the terrestrial nature of the great Saurian" (Owen, 1859)). Its placement as a valid genus remains controversial, with many authors preferring sinking the genus into *Varanus* (Molnar, 2004), which encompasses all living monitor lizards. The first aboriginal settlers of Australia would certainly have encountered living Megalania.

> Contents
> - Size of the Megalania
> - Live Megalania

## Size of the *Megalania*

Lack of enough fossil material has made it very hard to determine the exact dimensions of *Megalania*. (Molnar, 2004). Conservative estimates place the length of the largest individuals at a little over 7 meters (23 ft), with a maximum conservative weight of approximately 1940 kg (4,268 lbs [Molnar, 2004]). Average sized specimens would have been a leaner, but still impressive, 320 kg (704 lbs). *Megalania* was the largest land-dwelling lizard to have ever lived, and a fearsome predator as well as a scavenger. Judging from its size, *Megalania* would feed mostly on medium to large sized animals, including any of the giant marsupials like *Diprotodon* along with other reptiles, small mammals, and birds and their eggs and chicks. It had heavily built limbs and body and a large skull complete with a small crest in between the eyes, and a jaw full of serrated blade-like teeth. Due to its size and similarities to the Komodo Dragon, a relationship between the two species has been suggested. In reality however, Megalania's closest living relative is the perentie, Australia's largest living lizard, not the Komodo Dragon.

## Live *Megalania*

There have been numerous reports and rumors of living *Megalania* in Australia, and occasionally New Guinea, as recently as the mid 1990s. Australian cryptozoologist Rex Gilroy has stated that *Megalania* is still alive today, and it is only a matter of time until one comes in. Aside from stories and eyewitness accounts, the only suggestion that *Megalania* might still be alive today is plaster casts of possible *Megalania* footprints that Gilroy made in 1979. However, this view is not accepted by most scientists, and it has been pointed out that supposed sightings of this lizard did not begin until after its initial discovery.

In July 1734 a Norwegian missionary named Hans Egede, voyaging to Greenland, spotted something incredible as his vessel neared the Danish colony of Good Hope on the Davis Strait. "On the 6th," as he subsequently reported in straightforward terms,

> appeared a very terrible sea-animal, which raised itself so high above the water, that its head reached above our maintop. It had a long, sharp snout,

and blew like a whale, had broad, large flappers, and the body was, as it were, covered with a hard skin, and it was very wrinkled and uneven on its skin; moreover on the lower part it was formed like a snake, and when it went under water again, it cast itself backwards, and in doing so it raised its tail above the water, a whole ship-length from its body. That evening we had very bad weather.

*Missionary Hans Egede, a person of unquestioned integrity, supplied one of the earliest reliable firsthand accounts of a sea serpent, sighted near the coast of Greenland.*

*A 60-foot-long sea monster passed just yards from the H.M.S.* Daedalus, *according to Capt. Peter M'Quhae in his official report to the British admiralty.*

Maintaining its course to the southwest at a pace of 12 to 15 miles per hour, the creature passed the *Daedalus* rapidly but, stated M'Quhae, "so close under our lee quarter, that had it been a man of my acquaintance, I should easily have recognized his features with the naked eye."

A sea serpent of impressive size was reportedly seen in and around Gloucester Harbor, Massachusetts, by many persons during the month of August 1817. Prompted by heated debate between believers and skeptics, a special committee of the Linnaean Society of New England collected a sheaf of sworn statements from purported eyewitnesses. The affidavit of Matthew Gaffney, ship's carpenter, typically deposed:

> That on the 14th day of August. A.D. 1817, between the hours of four and five o'clock in the afternoon, I saw a strange marine animal, resembling a serpent in the harbor in said Gloucester. I was in a boat, and was within 30 feet of him. His head appeared full as large as a four-gallon keg, his body as large as a barrel, and his length that I saw I should judge 40 feet at least. The top of his head was of a dark color, and the underpart of his head appeared nearly white, as did also several feet of his belly that I saw . . . . I fired at him when he was the nearest to me.

The creature, Gaffney went on, turned as if to charge the boat, then sank like a stone and reappeared some 100 yards away. It moved at a rate of about one mile per two or three minutes.

Almost paralyzed by this apparition, Ridgway stopped rowing. After a moment he forced himself to turn and look for it. He saw nothing, but a few seconds later he heard "a most tremendous splash," as if the monster had surfaced and then crashed back into the sea. Ridgway was shaken. His account continues:

I am not an imaginative man, and I searched for a rational explanation. . . . Chay and I had seen whales and sharks, dolphins and porpoises, flying fish – all sorts of sea creatures but this monster in the night was none of these. I reluctantly had to believe that there was only one thing it could have been – a sea serpent.

Rightly expecting incredulity, Ridgway concluded: "I can only tell what I saw with my own eyes, and I am no longer a disbeliever."

*John Ridgway and Chay Blyth, who rowed across the Atlantic in the summer of 1966, were threatened by a sea serpent almost twice the length of their open boat, as depicted in this artist's rendition of the encounter.*

On April 26, 1890 the Tombstone Epitaph (a local Arizona newspaper) reported that two cowboys had discovered and shot down a creature – described as a "winged dragon" – which resembled a pterodactyl, only MUCH larger. The cowboys said its wingspan was 160 feet, and that its body was more than four feet wide and 92 feet long. The cowboys supposedly cut off the end of the wing to prove the existence of the creature. The paper's description of the animal fits the Quetzelcoatlus, whose fossils were found in Texas. (Gish, *Dinosaurs by Design*, 1992, p. 16.) Could this be thunderbird or Wakinyan, the jagged-winged, fierce-toothed flying creature of Sioux American Indian legend? This thunderbird supposedly live in a cave on the top of the Olympic Mountains and feasted on seafood. Different from the eagle (Wanbli) or hawk (Cetan) the Wakinyan was said to be huge, carrying off children, and was named because of its association with thunder and lightning – supposedly being struck by lightning and seen to fall to the ground during a storm. (Geis, Darlene, *Dinosaurs & Other Prehistoric Animals*, 1959, p. 9.) It was further distinguished by its piercing cry and thunderous beating wings (Lame Deer's 1969 interview).

In 2004 a fascinating dinosaur skull was donated to the Children's Museum of Indianapolis by three Sioux City, Iowa, residents who found it during a trip to the

Hell Creek Formation in South Dakota. The trio are still excavating the site, looking for more of the dinosaur's bones. Because of its dragon-like horns and teeth, the new species was dubbed Dracorex hogwartsia. This name honors the Harry Potter fictional works, which features the Hogwarts School and recently popularized dragons. The dinosaur's skull mixes spiky horns, bumps and a long muzzle. But unlike other members of the pachycephalosaur family, which have domed foreheads, this one is flat-headed. Consider some of the ancient stories of dragons, some fictional and some that might be authentic history of dinosaurs.

# Unicorns: Cryptids with One Horn

*The greater indian rhinoceros*

Tsintaosaurus

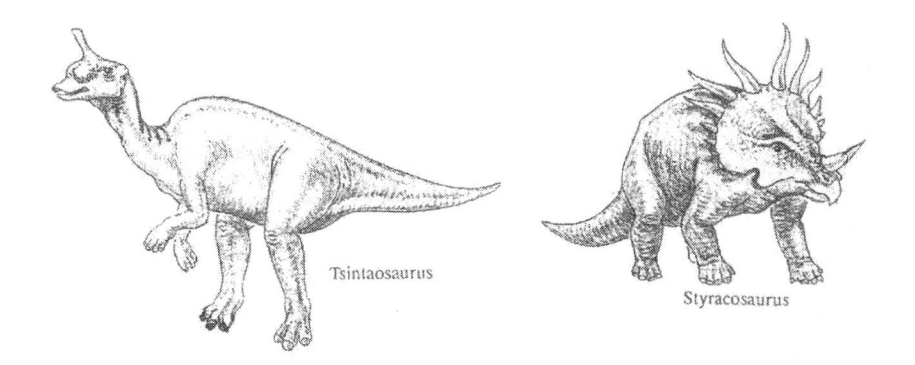

Styracosaurus

"WILL THE UNICORN be willing to serve thee, or abide by thy crib? Canst thou bind the unicorn with his band in the furrow? or will he harrow the valleys after thee? Wilt thou trust him, because his strength is great? or wilt thou leave thy labour to him? Wilt thou believe him, that he will bring home thy seed, and gather it into thy barn." Job 39:9-12

Unicorns were a strange animal described in ancient Greek and Roman myths. It was said to look much like a horse, except that on its forehad it had a single straight horn with a spiral twist. But the Bible never gives this description of a unicorn. The word "unicorn" means "one horn". Unicorn is mentioned 6 times in the Old Testament and unicorns is mentioned 3 times in the Old Testament. Neither one of them is mentioned in the New Testament.

There is a couple of dinosaurs that could of been called a unicorn because they possess one horn such as the "Styracasaurus" or the "Tsintaosaurus" or it could of been mistaking for a "Greater Indian Rhinoceros" that has one horn (which is only made of a mass of hair fibers and not of bone).

Unicorns did exist at one time because the Bible says so. Greek and Romans described the unicorn as having a white body, a red head and blue eyes. Its hind legs were like an antelopes and its tail like a lion's. The Bible describes its great strength in Numbers 23:22 and Numbers 24:8. In Job 39:9-12 tells how wild and ferocious it was. Even through the greater Indian rhinoceros has a fearsome appearance it is a generally peaceful animal.

The greater Indian rhino has a single, blunt, rather stubby horn, which is often ragged in older animals. It is made of a mass of hair-like fibers clumped together above a bony knob on the skull. The animal's thick, dark gray skin falls in distinct folds at the joints of the shoulders and flanks, giving an armored plate appearance.

## THE EMELA-NTOUKA OF THE CONGO

The same Likouala swamp region of the Congo which is supposed to be home to the Mokele-mbembe may also contain another dinosaurian: the Emela-ntouka (literally "killer of elephants"). This stout rhinoceros-like creature is reputed to have a penchant for killing elephants with its single horn.

Lucien Blancou, chief game inspector in French Equatorial Africa in the 1950's wrote of a ferocious creature, larger than a buffalo that was considered the most dangerous animal by the Kelle pygmies. ". . . the presence of a beast which sometimes disembowels elephants is also known, but it does not seem to be prevalent there now as in the preceding districts. A specimen was supposed to have been killed twenty years ago at Dongou, but on the left of the Ubangi and in the Belgian Congo." (translated by Heuvelmans, Bernard, *On the Track of Unknown Animals*, 1959.) In 1981 Dr. Roy Mackal traveled to the Congo searching for the rumored sauropod dinosaur Mokele-mbembe. But he was surprised to hear reports of another mysterious animal called the Emela-ntouka or "killer of elephants". The natives in the northwest region of the Likoula swamp told how it would gore elephants with its single horn. Mackal contemplation that it was a ceratopsian was cast in doubt by the pygmies not recollecting a neck frill. The description, however, does not fit a rhinoceros which has a short tail and does not have a true horn composed of bone or ivory. It is fused keratin (hair) and it seldom comes of the winner in a confrontation with elephants. Mackal left open the possibility that the Emela-ntouka was a Centrosaurus ("pointed lizard"). This member of the Ceratopsian family (formerly the Monoclonius) sports a single large horn on the center of its head as seen on right (Mackal, Roy, *A Living Dinosaur*, 1987, p. 247.). The ceratopsian identification has been strengthened by similar reports with a neck frill obtained by Genesis Park staff during a recent expedition to Cameroon. It also matches the classical authors' multiple references to a ferocious single-horned creature that spears elephants in the belly, and leaves them to bleed to death.

## STYRACOSAURUS

*Styracosaurus* (*sty-RACK-oh-SORE-us*) was called the "spiked lizard" because of the long spikes that stood up on the back end of his short frill. Perhaps he flaunted his massive head when he wanted control of the herd or when he was trying to attract a mate. Because several of the horned dinosaurs are so similar, some scientists have even wondered if the more ornamental frills were the males of the same species. Despite the fancy frill, his large nose horn was probably his best weapon; it stood straight up about 2 feet high and was 6 inches thick.

A mid-sized ceratopid, he weighed 3-4 tons, stood 6 feet tall, and stretched about 18 feet long. Despite his heavy body, he had only a short, thick tail. (Because quadrupeds walked on four legs, they did not need long tails for balancing.)

Fossil findings indicate that *Styracosaurus* cared for their young until they were fully grown.

# Tsintaosaurus

Pronunciation: SINT-ow-SAWR-us
Translation: Chinese Lizard, or Tsintao Lizard
Also Known As: Tanius
Description: Herbivore,
Bipedal
Order: Ornithischia
Suborder: Ornithopoda
Infraorder:
Iguanodontia
Family: Hadrosauridae
Height: 24 feet (7.3 meters)
Length: 33 feet (10 meters)

It was such a strange looking creature that for years some scientists thought that the horn was a mistake until another of these plant-eating duckbills was found with the same feature.

Like other duck-billed dinosaurs, Tsintaosaurus had hundreds of teeth packed closely together to form what is called a dental battery. These were used to grind tough plant fiber into mushy pulp.

Tsintaosaurus has caused no small amount of debate among scientists, partly due to the poor preservation of its skull. The exact position and function of its 'horn' are far from being agreed upon, despite the discovery of two partial skulls and remains of at least four individuals.

The German unicorn skeleton allegedly discovered in 1663 A unicorn skeleton was supposedly found at Einhornhöhle ("Unicorn Cave") in Germany's Harz Mountains in 1663.

Claims that the so-called unicorn had only two legs (and was constructed from fossil bones of mammoths and other animals) are contradicted or explained by accounts that souvenir-seekers plundered the skeleton; these accounts further claim that, perhaps remarkably, the souvenir-hunters left the skull, with horn.

# Beasts: Creatures of the Night

Revelation 9:1-12

1   AND the fifth angel sounded, and I saw a star fall from heaven unto the earth: and to him was given the key of the bottomless pit.
2   And he opened the bottomless pit; and there arose a smoke out of the pit, as the smoke of a great furnace; and the sun and the air were darkened by reason of the smoke of the pit.

3   And there came out of the smoke locusts upon the earth: and unto them was given power, as the scorpions of the earth have power.

4   And it was commanded them that they should not hurt the grass of the earth, neither any green thing, neither any tree; but only those men which have not the seal of God in their foreheads.

5   And to them it was given that they should not kill them, but that they should be tormented five months: and their torment *was* as the torment of a scorpion, when he striketh a man.

6   And in those days shall men seek death, and shall not find it; and shall desire to die, and death shall flee from them.

7   And the shapes of the locusts *were* like unto horses prepared unto battle; and on their heads *were* as it were crowns like gold, and their faces *were* as the faces of men.

8   And they had hair as the hair of women, and their teeth were as *the teeth* of lions.

9   And they had breastplates, as it were breastplates of iron; and the sound of their wings *was* as the sound of chariots of many horses running to battle.

10  And they had tails like unto scorpions, and there were stings in their tails: and their power *was* to hurt men five months.

11  And they had a king over them, *which* is the angel of the bottomless pit, whose name in the Hebrew tongue *is* A-bad'-don, but in the Greek tongue hath *his* name A-pol'-ly-on.

12  One woe is past: *and*, behold, there come two woes more hereafter.

THE CREATURES THAT fall in this category are most elusive of all. Revelation 9:1-12 describes cryptids that have not yet been seen on the Earth. They will be released during the Great Tribulation Period and will plague men who are left on the Earth for 5 months. Darkness will come to the Earth when the pit (another dimension) is open and the smoke ascends out of the pit that is bottomless to darken the Sun and the atmosphere of the Earth. The beasts (locusts with scorpion tails) will be in this smoke. This swarm of cryptids will go with the other cryptids that are already on the Earth such as the unicorns, dragons and satyrs that are described in Isaiah 34:7, 13-15.

But until this day comes there has been and will continue to come many beasts (creatures of the night) such as the Jersey Devil, Mothman, Kongamato, Bigfoot, Sasquatch, Abominable Snowman and many more. Even if these creatures are a myth (which I think they are not) they tend to be seen in the night and can change shape and appear and disappear at any moment of time.

In New Jersey there have been periodic reports of the Jersey Devil as noted in Janet and Colin Bord's *Alien Animals*. This improbable critter, said by some to be the size of a large crane, is variously described as having a long, thick neck; long back legs with cloven hooves; short front legs with paws; batlike wings with about a two-foot spread; the head of a horse, dog, or ram; and a long, scrawny tail.

In his book *In Witchbound Africa*, Frank H. Melland reports hearing repeatedly of a fearful creature called the Kongamato that resembles a flying lizard with smooth skin, a beak full of teeth, and wings with batlike skin and a span of four to seven feet. This sounds suspiciously like a cousin of the pterodactyl.

Those who tell of seeing Kongamato or the Jersey Devil are doubtless sincere about it. The sightings are currently too few to build a convincing case. But should they become as frequent as those of Nessie and the Sasquatch, we will have airborne candidates for the Society of Probable Monsters (SOPM).

From places as far removed as Washington, Texas, and West Virginia have come reports of Mothman, as noted in John A. Keel's book *The Mothman Prophecies*. This strange, winged creature is reputed to be man-shaped and gray in color, which accounts for the name. Most people who say they have seen it agree that it emanates an aura of bone-chilling fear. One witness, confessing to unreasonable terror during his encounter

*This illustration of a "Jersey Devil," reported in 1909 by a couple living in Gloucester, New Jersey, appeared in a Philadelphia newspaper story about the sighting.*

## The Swarm

Description of the locusts that God has created to be used in the Great Tribulation for five months in the Fifth trumpet judgment against man on the Earth. These locusts will have a king over them and his name is called Abaddon in the Hebrew and Apollyon in the Greek. (Revelation 9:11)

1. Shape of the locusts: like unto horses prepared unto battle (Rev. 9:7)
2. On their heads: crowns like gold (Rev. 9:7)
3. Faces: like faces of men (Rev. 9:7)
4. Hair: like hair of women (Rev. 9:8)
5. Teeth: like teeth of lions (Rev. 9:8)
6. Breastplates: like breastplates of iron (Rev. 9:9)
7. Wings: (Rev. 9:9)
8. Tails: tails like scorpions (stings in their tails) (Rev. 9:10)

# Fiery Flying Serpents: Flying Reptiles

"THE BURDEN OF the beasts of the south: into the land of trouble and anguish, from whence come the young and old lion, the viper and fiery flying serpent, they will carry their riches upon the shoulders of young asses, and their treasures upon the bunches of camels, to a people that shall not profit them." Isaiah 30:6

In Isaiah chapter 30 verse 6 the Bible talks about fiery flying serpents. The color of these serpents with wings were reddish copper. The Hebrew word used for fiery is "saraph" which means copper color. There has been reports out of Africa and Arabia of small reddish flying reptiles. The Greek explorer Herodotus also described these creatures which sound amazingly like the small "Rhamphorhynchus". They had the same snakelike body and bat-like wings. Many of these creatures had been killed near the city of Buto (Arabia). Herodotus was taken to a canyon were he seen many piles of skeletons of these creatures. Herodotus was amazed at seeing them in the spice groves in large numbers. Aristotle a well respected Greek philosopher said that in his time these creatures were known to exist in Ethiopia. Similiar animals about 3 feet long were also described by geographer Strabo to live in India. In the Arabian Sea region here have been sightings of these creatures. They call them "Arabhar". Closer to home there was a sighting of one of these fiery flying serpent in Zionsville, Indiana.

*Rhamphorhynchus* was a long-tailed pterosaur of the Jurassic period. Its name means 'beak jaw'. Only 17.5 cm (7 in) long but with a wingspan of 100 cm (3 ft), it was less specialized than the later pterodactyloids. It had a long tail stiffened with ligaments which ended in a diamond-shaped vane.

> *Rhamphorhynchus muensteri* –
> Oxford University Museum of
> Natural History.

Rhamphorhynchus probably ate fish and it is believed that one of the ways it hunted was by dragging its beak in the water, catching fish and tossing them into its throat pouch, a structure similar to that of pelicans, which has been preserved in some fossils. This method of catching fish is found today in skimmers.

Although fossils have been found in England, the best preserved come from the Solnhofen quarry in Bavaria; many of these fossils preserve not only the bones but impressions of soft tissue.

| | |
|---|---|
| \multicolumn{2}{c}{Rhamphorhynchus} |
| \multicolumn{2}{c}{Rhamphorhynchus gemmingi} |
| \multicolumn{2}{c}{Conservation status} |
| \multicolumn{2}{c}{Extinct (fossil)} |
| \multicolumn{2}{c}{Scientific classification} |
| Kingdom: | Animalia |
| Phylum: | Chordata |
| Class: | Sauropsida |
| Order: | Pterosauria |
| Suborder: | Rhamphorhynchoidea |
| Family: | Rhamphorhynchidae |
| Genus: | Rhamphorhynchus |
| \multicolumn{2}{c}{Species} |
| \multicolumn{2}{l}{R. muensteri} |
| \multicolumn{2}{l}{R. gemmingi} |
| \multicolumn{2}{l}{R. longiceps} |

# KONGAMATO

A flying reptile with smooth skin, a beak full of teeth, and wings with batlike skin and a span of four to seven feet. They are a type of pterosaur seen throughout sub-Saharan Africa.

The flying serpent got its first Western attention when Frank H. Melland wrote about it in his book "In Witchbound Africa" in 1923. when Melland asked local inhabitants about the Kongamato, he was told it was a flying animal with membranes on its wings instead of feathers, teeth in its mouth, generally red in color, and from four to seven feet across the wings. Frank showed them a picture of an extinct pterodactyl, and the locals identified it as a Kongamato.

Another account of pterosaur-like flying monsters came from the distinguished British newspaper correspondent G. Ward Price. Mr. Price was with the future Duke of Windsor in Southren Rhodesia in 1925 when they learned of the recent attacks of one of these creatures on a local man in a swamp. Here again, shown a book of animals, the man picked out the pterosaur.

AFRICAN PTEROSAUR

# Timeline

| | | |
|---|---|---|
| 4004 B.C. | – | Creation of sea, flying, land animals and man by God of the Bible (from the Masoretic text; Book of Genesis). |
| 1520 B.C. | – | Unicorn, Behemoth, and Leviathan described in the Book of Job. |
| 712 B.C. | – | Satyrs and Fiery Flying Serpents described in the Book of Isaiah. |
| 588 B.C. | – | Dragon mentioned in the Book of Ezekiel. |
| 456 B.C. | – | Herodotus, a Greek explorer described Ramphorhychus from his eyewitness account. |
| 200 A.D. | – | Roman mosaics showed two-long necked dragons fighting. |
| 300 A.D. | – | The men of Alexander the Great were scared to death of dragons. |
| 1000 A.D. | – | Vikings had dragon heads on the front of their ships. |
| 1572 | – | An Italian peasant killed a dragon. A scientist documented it. |
| 1817-1819 | – | New England (Gloucester) Sea Serpent sightings peaked. (about 100 sightings) |
| 1841 | – | The word "dinosaur" was invented by Sir Richard Owen. (before that time they were called dragons) |
| 1890 | – | Two cowboys shot and killed a flying reptile near Tombstone, Arizona. |
| 1907 | – | Col. Percy Fawcett saw a Diplodocus in the Amazon jungle. |
| 1909 | – | Over 1,000 Jersey Devil sightings reported. |
| 1910 | – | The New York Herald ran a story: "Is Brontosaurus roaming Africa wilds?" |
| 1912 | – | First Komodo Dragon captured. |
| 1913 | – | First Mokele-Mbembe expedition to Africa. |
| 1920 | – | The term "Sasquatch" is invented by J.W. Burns. |
| 1921 | – | The word "Abominable Snowman coined by Henry Newman. |

|  |  |
|---|---|
| 1924 | – Ape Canyon Incident: several miners were attacked after firing on a Sasquatch near Mt. Saint Helens, Oregon. |
| 1933 | – Loch Ness Monster sightings begin. |
| | – Cadborosaurus name is selected by newspaper contest. Creature is called "Caddy" for short. |
| 1937 | – Caddy corpse is found in a stomach of a sperm whale. |
| 1938 | – First Coelacanth is captured off the coast of South Africa. |
| 1947 | – Sea monster carcass found on a beach near Effingham on Vancouver Island. |
| 1948 | – The Saturday Evening Post said, "There Could Be Dinosaurs". |
| 1952 | – Second Coelacanth captured. |
| 1958 | – The name "Bigfoot" invented when a Bluff Creek Valley area construction worker unveils a plaster cast of the monster's footprint. |
| 1959 | – A 42-year veteran missionary Eugene Thomas knew of two church men who killed a Mokele-Mbembe. |
| | – The term "Cryptozoology" is invented. |
| 1967 | – The Patterson-Gimlin film of Bigfoot is shot. |
| 1977 | – Sandra Mansi takes photograph of "Champ". |
| 1979 | – Plaster cast made of a footprint of a live Megalania by Roy Gilroy. |
| 1980 | – Dr. Roy Mackal headed an expedition to the Congo in search of Mokele-Mbembe. |
| 1982 | – Legislation is passed making it unlawful to harm Champ. |
| 1983 | – The term "Cryptid" invented by John E. Wall. |
| 1997 | – Indonesian Coelacanth captured. |
| 2000 | – Cancer survivor Daryl Ellis attempts to swim Lake Okanagan and sees "Ogopogo". |
| 2006 | – Sighting of a "Rhamporhynchus" in Zionsville, Indiana. |

# Add With All Diligence These Seven Outgrowths of Faith

"SIMON PETER, A servant and an apostle of Jesus Christ, to them that have obtained like precious faith with us through the righteousness of God and our Saviour Jesus Christ: Grace and peace be multiplied unto you through the knowledge of God, and of Jesus our Lord, According as his divine power hath given unto us all things that pertain unto life and godliness, through the knowledge of him that hath called us to glory and virtue: Whereby are given unto us exceeding great and precious promises: that by these ye might be partakers of the divine nature, having escaped the corruption that is in the world through lust. And beside this, giving all diligence, add to your faith virtue; and to virtue knowledge; And to knowledge temperance; and to temperance patience; and to patience godliness; And to godliness brotherly kindness; and to brotherly kindness charity. For if these things be in you, and abound, they make you that ye shall neither be barren nor unfruitful in the knowledge of our Lord Jesus Christ. But he that lacketh these things is blind, and cannot see afar off, and hath forgotten that he was purged from his old sins. Wherefore the rather brethren, give diligence to make your calling and election sure: for if ye do these things, ye shall never fall: For so an entrance shall be ministered unto you abundantly into the everlasting kingdom of our Lord and Saviour Jesus Christ." (II Peter 1:1-11)

The Apostle Peter starts out by saying, "to them that have obtained like precious faith with us through the righteousness of God and our Saviour Jesus Christ." Then he lists the seven outgrowths of this faith that we are to give all diligence to build us into solid and successful Christians when we make them part of our lives.

FAITH: It all starts with faith in the Lord Jesus Christ as personal Saviour. Knowing Him you will begin to live up to God's potential for you.

FAITH (definition): Belief, trust, confidence; conviction in regard to religion; system of religious beliefs; strict adherence to duty and promises; word or honor pledged.

> "For by grace are ye saved through faith; and that not of yourselves: it is the gift of God: Not of works, lest any man should boast. For we are his workmanship, created in Christ Jesus unto good works, which God hath before ordained that we should walk in them." (Ephesians 2:8-10)

> "So then faith cometh by hearing, and hearing by the word of God." (Romans 10:17)

> "Now faith is the substance of things hoped for, the evidence of things not seen." (Hebrews 11:1)

> "But without faith it is impossible to please him: for he that cometh to God must believe that he is, and that he is a rewarder of them that diligently seek him." (Heb. 11:6)

## ADD TO YOUR FAITH:

1. VIRTUE: Is doing the right thing as a pattern in life. It gives you credibility among the people you meet.

   VIRTUE (definition): Moral goodness, rectitude, morality; chastity, merit; efficacy.

   Scripture: "Finally, brethren, whatsoever things are true, whatsoever things are honest, whatsoever things are just, whatsoever things are pure, whatsoever things are lovely, whatsoever things are of good report; if there be any virtue, and if there be any praise, think on these things." (Philippians 4:8)

2. KNOWLEDGE (WISDOM): Is one of the pillars mentioned in Proverbs. "Wisdom hath builded her house, she hath hewn out her seven pillars." (Proverbs 9:1) A commitment to growth in knowledge, first the basics of the faith and then the deeper doctrines, enables us to exercise wisdom in life's choices.

KNOWLEDGE (definition): The result or condition of knowing; clear perception; learning; information; skill; acquintance.

Scripture: "The fear of the LORD is the beginning of knowledge: but fools despise wisdom and instruction." (Proverbs 1:7)

Scripture: "Give instruction to a wise man, and he will be yet wiser: teach a just man, and he will increase in learning." (Proverbs 9:9)

Scripture: "The fear of the LORD is the beginning of wisdom: and the knowledge of the holy is understanding." (Proverbs 9:10)

Scripture: "But grow in grace, and in the knowledge of our Lord and Saviour Jesus Christ. To him be glory both now and for ever. Amen." (II Peter 3:18)

3. TEMPERANCE (SELF-CONTROL): God wants you to be in control of yourself, and will enable you to do so victoriously. You need control of your actions – emotions, physical state etc. People who are under addiction from illicit drugs, alcohol, tobacco etc. have no self-control. Take these chemicals away from them and their anger and anxiety builds. Addictions are very dangerous because the body craves these chemicals more and more each time to get the same effect. Eventually death occurs from the damage of these poisons.

TEMPERANCE (definition): Moderation in indulgence of natural appetites, sobriety; abstinence from intoxicants.

Scripture: "He that is slow to anger is better than the mighty; and he that ruleth his spirit than he that taketh a city." (Proverbs 16:32)

Scripture: "He that hath no rule over his own spirit is like a city that is broken down, and without walls." (Proverbs 25:28)

Scripture: "Know ye not that they which run in a race run all, but one receiveth the prize? So run, that ye may obtain. And every man that striveth for the mastery is temperate in all things. Now they do it to obtain a corruptible crown; but we an incorruptible. I therefore so run, not as uncertainly; so fight I, not as one that beateth the air: But I keep under my body, and bring it into subjection: lest that by any means, when I have preached to others, I myself should be a castaway." (I Corinthians 9:24-27)

4. PATIENCE (PERSEVERANCE): The ability to bear trials without grumbling. To abide under. God tells us to hold up to our responsibilities, to be dependable and never run away from the things we are supposed to do.

   PATIENCE (definition): Quality of being patient; endurance, composure, forbearance.

   Scripture: "Behold, we count them happy which endure. Ye have heard of the patience of Job, and have seen the end of the Lord; that the Lord is very pitiful, and of tender mercy." (James 5:11)

   Scripture: "He that is slow to wrath is of great understanding: but he that is hasty of spirit exalteth folly." (Proverbs 14:29)

   Scripture: "Better is the end of a thing than the beginning thereof: and the patient in spirit is better than the proud in spirit." (Ecclesiastes 7:8)

   Scripture: "Blessed is the man that endureth temptation: for when he is tried, he shall receive the crown of life, which the Lord hath promised to them that love him." (James 1:12)

   Scripture: "For this is thankworthy, if a man for conscience toward God endure grief, suffering wrongfully. For what glory is it, if, when ye be buffeted for your faults, ye shall take it patiently? but if, when ye do well, and suffer for it, ye take it patiently, this is acceptable with God." (I Peter 2:19-20)

5. GODLINESS: Which means that in every circumstance, we should ask, "What should I do as a representative of God? We are to have reverence for God.

   GODLINESS (definition): Quality of being godly; piety; reverence for God.

   Scripture: "Wherefore we receiving a kingdom which cannot be moved, let us have grace, whereby we may serve God acceptably with reverence and godly fear: For our God is a consuming fire." (Hebrews 12:28-29)

6. BROTHERLY KINDNESS: Kindness to others is upmost important especially to people who are in need. We are to have a friendly attitude towards others.

KINDNESS: (definition): Quality and state of being kind; benevolence; a kind act.

Scripture: "Be kindly affectioned one to another with brotherly love; in honour preferring one another." (Romans 12:10)

Scripture: "Let all bitterness, and wrath, and anger, and clamour, and evil speaking, be put away from you, with all malice: And be ye kind one to another, tenderhearted, forgiving one another, even as God for Christ's sake hath forgiven you." (Eph. 4:31-32)

7. CHARITY (LOVE): It is one of the chief identifying characteristics of the Christian life. It is a genuine and unselfish concern for others. It is not erotic but agape type love. An attribute of God: ". . . for God is love." (I John 4:8)

CHARITY (definition): A disposition to relieve the wants of others. alms.

LOVE (definition): To regard with affection; to like; to delight in.

Scripture: "If ye fulfil the royal law according to the scripture, Thou shalt love thy neighbour as thyself, ye do well: (James 2:8)

Scripture: "Put on therefore, as the elect of God, holy and beloved, bowels of mercies, kindness, humbleness of mind, meekness, longsuffering; Forbearing one another, and forgiving one another, if any man have a quarrel against any: even as Christ forgave you, so also do ye. And above all these things put on charity, which is the bond of perfectness." (Colossians 3:12-14)

# Why I Believe and Contend for the Creation Account

1. Created in 6 literal (24 hour) days by our Lord Jesus Christ:

   Scriptures: (Genesis 1:1-31), (Genesis 2:1-3), (Exodus 20:11), (Exodus 31:17) (Colossians 1:12-18)

2. Relatively young Earth:

   Scriptures: (Exodus 20:11), (Exodus 31:17), (Leviticus 23:3), (II Peter 3:8)

   6 days of Creation + 1 day rested = 7 days: correlates with 6,000 years man will be on the Earth before the last 1,000 years called the thousand year reign of Jesus Christ (Revelation 20:1-8). The Earth will be 6,000 years old when it goes into the millennial reign of Jesus Christ.

3. Eve – "mother of all living" (humans):

   Scriptures: (Genesis 2:21-23), (Genesis 3:20)

4. Adam – first man God created from the dust of the ground:

   Scriptures: (Genesis 2:7), (I Corinthians 15:45a), (I Corinthians 15:47a) (I Timothy 2:13)

5. True doctrine (from God's Word): Jesus spoke of His Creation when He walked the Earth (Mark 10:6) and God cannot lie (Heb. 6:17-20).

6. In a orderly fashion and out of nothing God created everything that exists:

   Scriptures: (Isaiah 45:18), (John 1:1-3), (I Corinthians 14:33, 40), (Colossians 1:12-17), (Hebrews 11:1-3)

7. Only believed through faith in the Word of God:

   Scripture: (Hebrews 11:3)

8. No room for Gap theory between Genesis 1:1 & 1:2:

   Genesis 1:1 & 1:2 are connected and are part of the first day of Creation (Genesis 1:1-5). The Earth was without form and void before God started His creative processes on it.

# Creation 101

"The heavens declare the glory of God; and the firmament sheweth his handywork. Day unto day uttereth speech, and night unto night sheweth knowledge. There is no speech nor language, where their voice is not heard." (Psalm 19:1-3)

"He hath made the earth by his power, he hath established the world by his wisdom, and hath stretched out the heavens by his discretion." (Jeremiah 10:12)

"For the invisible things of him from the creation of the world are clearly seen, being understood by the things that are made, even his eternal power and Godhead; so that they are without excuse." (Romans 1:20)

WELCOME TO CREATION 101 and the following irrefutable facts from the Holy Scriptures contained in the Word of God (KJV).

1. The first three verses of Genesis accurately express all known aspects of the creation account. "In the beginning God created the heaven and the earth. And the earth was without form, and void; and darkness was upon the face of the deep. And the Spirit of God moved upon the face of the waters. And God said, Let there be light: and there was light."

    Science expresses the universe in terms of: time, space, matter, and energy. In Genesis chapter one we read: "In the beginning (time) God

created the heaven (space) and the earth (matter) . . . Then God said, "Let there be light (energy)."
2. The earth is a sphere (Isaiah 40:22) Eventhough at one time people thought the earth was flat, the Bible told us that the earth is spherical.
3. Creation is made of particles, indiscernible to our eyes Hebrews 11:3). It was not until the 19th century that scientists discovered that all visible matter consists of invisible elements called atoms.
4. The earth was designed for biological life (Isaiah 45:18). Scientists have discovered that the most fundamental characteristics of our earth and universe are so finely tuned that if just one of them were even slightly different, life as we know it could not exist.
5. Light travels in a path (Job 38:19). Light is said to have a "way". We know now that light is a form of energy that travels at 186,000 miles per second in a straight line. Like the Bible says there is a "way" of light. Light can be divided (Job 38:24). Sir Isaac Newton studied light and discovered that white light is made of seven colors, which can be parted and then recombined. Light also can be sent, and then manifest itself in speech (Job 38:35). We now know that radio waves and light waves are two forms of the same thing called electromagnetic waves. Therefore, radio waves are a form of light. Today, using radio transmitters, we can send "lightnings" which indeed speak when they arrive.
6. Each star is unique (I Corinthians 15:41). Long before the invention of the telescope, the Bible declared that each star created by God varies in size and intensity!
7. The First Law of Thermodynamics established (Genesis 2:1-2). This law states that the total amount of energy and matter in the universe is a constant. One form of energy or matter may be converted into another, but the total quantity always remains the same. Therefore the creation is finished, exactly as God said it was way back in Genesis.

# FIRST DAY OF CREATION

1  IN the beginning God created the heaven and the earth.
2  And the earth was without form, and void; and darkness *was* upon the face of the deep. And the Spirit of God moved upon the face of the waters.
3  And God said, Let there be light: and there was light.
4  And God saw the light, that *it was* good: and God divided the light from the darkness.
5  And God called the light Day, and the darkness he called Night. And the evening and the morning were the first day.

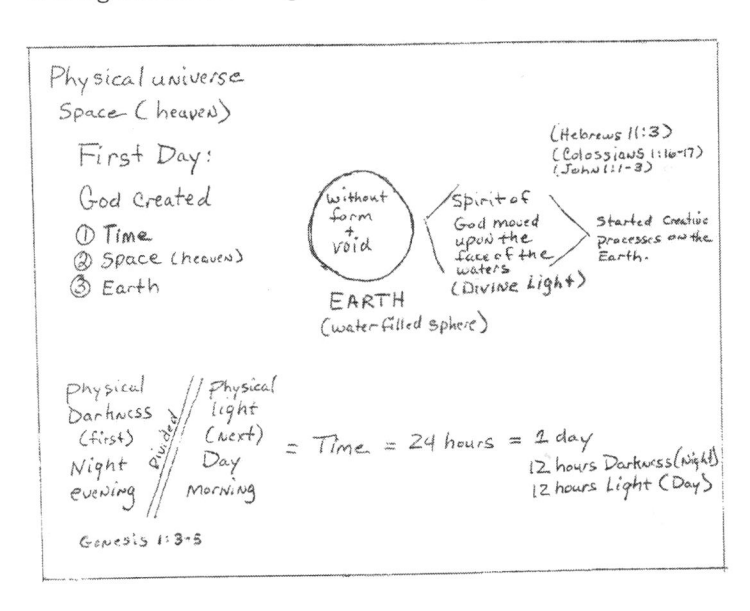

```
Physical universe
Space (heaven)                                    (Hebrews 11:3)
                                                  (Colossians 1:16-17)
First Day:                                        (John 1:1-3)
God created          Without    Spirit of
                     form       God moved       Started Creative
 ① Time              +          upon the        processes on the
 ② Space (heaven)    void       face of the     Earth.
 ③ Earth                        waters
                                (Divine Light)
                     EARTH
                     (water-filled sphere)

Physical  // Physical
Darkness  // light
(first)   // (next)     = Time = 24 hours = 1 day
Night     // Day                  12 hours Darkness (Night)
evening   // Morning              12 hours Light (Day)

Genesis 1:3-5
```

1. Genesis 1:1 God created physical space (heaven: universe) and a physical Earth. They were both created right after time was created.
2. Genesis 1:2 The Earth had no physical features on it. It was just a sphere of water and the space (universe) He created had nothing in it but the Earth. It was dark until the Spirit of God moved upon the face of the waters. Jesus Christ was the Light that shined in this darkness (John 1:5) until He created physical light on Day Four of Creation Week.

THE FIRST BOOK OF MOSES, CALLED<br>GENESIS

# SECOND DAY OF CREATION

6   And God said, Let there be a firmament in the midst of the waters, and let it divide the waters from the waters.
7   And God made the firmament, and divided the waters which *were* under the firmament from the waters which *were* above the firmament: and it was so.
8   And God called the firmament Heaven. And the evening and the morning were the second day.

1. Genesis 1:6-8 God created an atmosphere around the Earth. He divided the waters under the firmament (Earth: water sphere) from the waters above the firmament (water canopy). He called the firmament Heaven (atmosphere).
2. We know through the Scriptures that there is three heavens. First heaven is the atmosphere around the Earth. The second heaven is outerspace or the universe outside the Earth's atmosphere. The third heaven is God's abode. Paul, an apostle of the Lord Jesus Christ was taken up to the third heaven in II Corinthians 12:2.

# THIRD DAY OF CREATION

9   And God said, Let the waters under the heaven be gathered together unto one place, and let the dry *land* appear: and it was so.
10  And God called the dry *land* Earth, and the gathering together of the waters called he Seas; and God saw that *it was* good.
11  And God said, Let the earth bring forth grass, the herb yielding seed, *and* the fruit tree yielding fruit after his kind, whose seed *is* in itself, upon the earth: and it was so.
12  And the earth brought forth grass, *and* herb yielding seed after his kind, and the tree yielding fruit, whose seed *was* in itself, after his kind: and God saw that *it was* good.
13  And the evening and the morning were the third day.

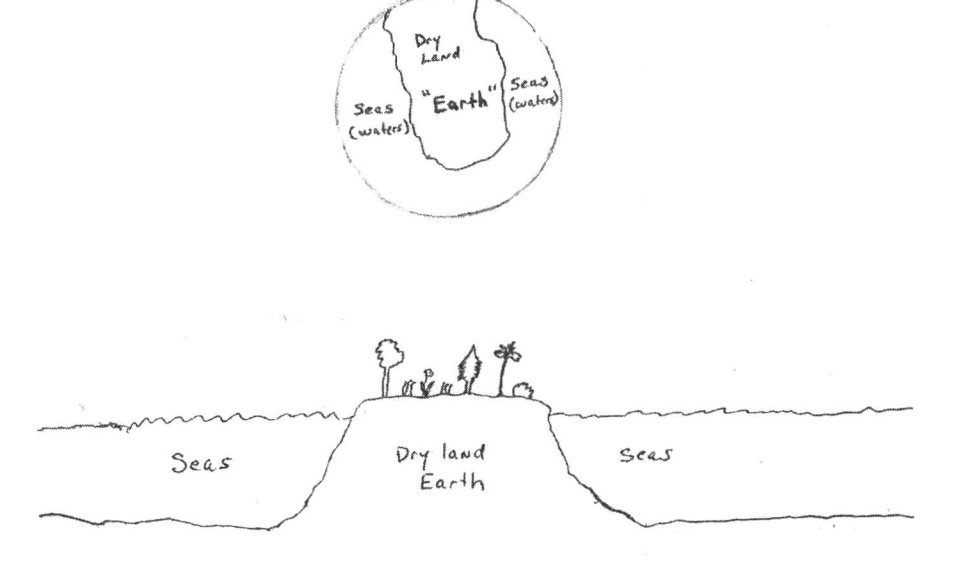

1. Genesis 1:9-13 God gathered the waters together in one place and called them Seas. And the dry land that appeared He called Earth. He then created plant life (grass, herb yielding seed, fruit trees, etc.).

## FOURTH DAY OF CREATION

14 And God said, Let there be lights in the firmament of the heaven to divide the day from the night; and let them be for signs, and for seasons, and for days, and years:

15 And let them be for lights in the firmament of the heaven to give light upon the earth: and it was so.

16 And God made two great lights; the greater light to rule the day, and the lesser light to rule the night: *he made* the stars also.

17 And God set them in the firmament of the heaven to give light upon the earth,

18 And to rule over the day and over the night, and to divide the light from the darkness: and God saw that *it was* good.

19 And the evening and the morning were the fourth day.

1. Genesis 1:14-19 God created physical light. The Sun (greater light) to rule the day. The moon (lesser light) to rule the night. The moon reflects the light from the Sun. God also created the stars at this time. They were created for signs (not to be mistaken for Astrology-the worship of stars and other heavenly bodies) These signs were constellations that were formed by these stars such as Orion (Job 38:31), (Amos 5:8) Gemini (Castor and Pollux: Acts 28:11). These lights were also created for seasons (winter, spring, summer, fall), for days, and for years.

2. God positioned our Earth far enough away from the Sun (third from from the sun).

## FIFTH DAY OF CREATION

20 And God said, Let the waters bring forth abundantly the moving creature that hath life, and fowl *that* may fly above the earth in the open firmament of heaven.
21 And God created great whales, and every living creature that moveth, which the waters brought forth abundantly, after their kind, and every winged fowl after his kind: and God saw that *it was* good.
22 And God blessed them, saying, Be fruitful, and multiply, and fill the waters in the seas, and let fowl multiply in the earth.
23 And the evening and the morning were the fifth day.

1. Genesis 1:20-23 God created sea creatures (fishes, whales, coelacanths, plesiosaurs, jellyfishes, octopuses, etc) to move about in the waters. He created the birds and flying reptiles (dove, raven, eagle, pteranodons, etc) to fly above in the earth's atmosphere.

## SIX DAY OF CREATION

24 And God said, Let the earth bring forth the living creature after his kind, cattle, and creeping thing, and beast of the earth after his kind: and it was so.
25 And God made the beast of the earth after his kind, and cattle after their kind, and every thing that creepeth upon the earth after his kind: and God saw that *it was* good.
26 And God said, Let us make man in our image, after our likeness: and let them have dominion over the fish of the sea, and over the fowl of the air, and over the cattle, and over all the earth, and over every creeping thing that creepeth upon the earth.
27 So God created man in his own image, in the image of God created he him; male and female created he them.
28 And God blessed them, and God said unto them, Be fruitful, and multiply, and replenish the earth, and subdue it: and have dominion over the fish of the sea, and over the fowl of the air; and over every living thing that moveth upon the earth.
29 And God said, Behold, I have given you every herb bearing seed, which *is* upon the face of all the earth, and every tree, in the which is the fruit of a tree yielding seed; to you it shall be for meat.
30 And to every beast of the earth, and to every fowl of the air, and to every thing that creepeth upon the earth, wherein *there is* life, I *have given* every green herb for meat: and it was so.
31 And God saw every thing that he had made, and, behold, *it was* very good. And the evening and the morning were the sixth day.

1. Genesis 1:24-31 God created the land animals (mammals, reptiles, amphibians, insects, arachnids, dinosaurs, etc).
   God created man (Adam) then woman (Eve) from Adam's rib (Genesis 2:21-25 to take care of what God created.
2. Genesis 2:1-2 God created for His purpose and pleasure (Revelation 4:11) and ended His work on the seventh day. And everything that God made was very good.

1 THUS the heavens and the earth were finished, and all the host of them.
2 And on the seventh day God ended his work which he had made; and he rested on the seventh day from all his work which he had made.

# The Gap Theory: Is it Scriptural?

"In the beginning God created the heaven and the earth. And the earth was without form, and void; and darkness was upon the face of the deep. And the Spirit of God moved upon the face of the waters." (Genesis 1:1-2)

THERE HAS BEEN many people who have tried to place a gap between Genesis chapter one verses one and two. They state that there is a gap of indeterminate time between these two Scriptures. There is many different versions as to what supposedly happened in this "gap" of time. Most of versions state that the "GAP THEORY" places millions of years of geological time (includes billions of fossil remains) in between these two first verses of Genesis. This version is also called the "RUIN – RECONSTRUCTION THEORY".

W.W. Fields from his book "Unformed and Unfilled" gives a summary of what the gap theory is: "In the far distant dateless past, God created a perfect heaven and perfect earth. Satan was ruler of the earth which was peopled by a race of men without any souls. Eventually, Satan, who dwelled in a garden of Eden composed of minerals rebelled by desiring to become like God. Because of Satan's fall, sin entered the universe and brought on the earth God's judgment in the form of a flood (indicated by the water of Genesis 1:2), and then a global ice age when the light and heat from the sun were somehow removed. All the plant, animal, and human fossils upon the earth today date from this "Lucifer's flood" and do not bear any genetic relationship with the plants, animals, and humans living upon the earth today."

Some versions of the gap theory state that the fossil record (geologic column) formed over millions of years, and then God destroyed the earth with a catastrophe (Lucifer's flood) that left it "without form and void."

In the 19th century, it became popular to believe that the geological changes occurred slowly, and roughly at the present rate (UNIFORMITARIANISM). With increased acceptance of uniformitarianism, many theologians urged reinterpretation of Genesis (with ideas such as DAY-AGE THEORY, PROGRESSIVE CREATION THEORY, THEISTIC EVOLUTION THEORY, DAYS-OF-REVELATION THEORY).

The term "UNIFORMITARIAN" commonly refers to the idea that geological processes such as erosion and sedimentation have remained essentially the same throughout time, and so the present is the key to the past. But after the mid-19th century, the concept has been extended. Huxley said, "Consistent uniformitarianism postulates evolution as much in the organic as in the inorganic world."

C. I. Scofield D.D. (Doctor of Divinity) who was a Freemason states in his footnotes: "That Genesis 1:1 is the first creative act that refers to the dateless past, and gives scope for all the geological ages. He also states that Genesis 1:2 along with Jeremiah 4:23-26, Isaiah 24:1, Isaiah 45:18, clearly indicate that the earth had undergone a cataclysmic change as the result of a divine judgment. the face of the earth bears everywhere the marks of such a catastrophe." (The Scofield Study Bible) Other notable people who believed in the gap theory are as follows: William Buckland, G.H. Pember, Arthur C. Custance, William Conybeare, Hugh Miller, just to name a few.

But the most notable of all and perhaps the man most responsible for the "GAP THEORY" is Thomas Chalmers (1780-1847). He was a Scottish theologian and first moderator of the Free Church of Scotland.

In 1803 in one of his lectures at Saint Andrews he stated that, "The writings of Moses do not fix the antiquity of the globe. If they fix anything at all, it is only the antiquity of the species." Dr. William Buckland, a geologist adopted this view from Chalmers on the interpretation of the first two verses of Genesis.

Most of the men who believed in the Gap Theory did not believe in the worldwide Noahaic Flood. They said the flood was only of local geographic extent.

Hugh Miller (1802-1856) a 19th century Scottish geologist in his book, "The Testimony of the Rocks" gives lectures on this. Although he claimed to be a creationist, Miller did not believe in a global Noahaic Flood. He believed that the flood was of only local extent, probably somewhere in the Middle East or Central Asia. He also believed in a "DAY-AGE" theory. Miller equated the biblical "day" with an indefinite period of time and identified specific geological eras with the "days" in Genesis, such as DAY THREE was the Palezoic era, DAY FIVE was the Secondary, and DAY SIX was the Tertiary. In his fourth lecture "THE MOSAIC VISION OF CREATION" he states this very thing. The story of Miller ends on a tragic note. He died at his own hands (suicide) in 1856, after a long but episodic period of "illness of the brain", apparently aggravated by the stress of writing his final work "The Testimony of the Rocks".

## *EXPOSING THE GAP THEORY FOR WHAT IT IS*

1. *IN THE BEGINNING*: Thus saith the Lord from His Word (KJV).

These first three words "In the beginning" tells us when God started His physical creative acts. Our God is Eternal and what He created first was time. There is no time in God's abode. He created time for man. "In the beginning" is the start of our physical universe called outerspace (heaven) and our physical planet called earth.

The Scripture clearly states that our God the Lord Jesus Christ is a God of order. He does everything decently and in order (I Corinthians 14:40). He first created a physical universe called heaven, then He created a physical sphere called Earth to be put in that physical universe. "In the beginning God created the heaven and the earth." (Genesis 1:1).

There is no gap between Genesis 1:1 and 1:2. Because in Genesis 1:2 the Scripture states that the Earth was a sphere without form and void. It was a sphere that was covered with water. This is showing what the Earth look like before God started His creative acts on it. Genesis 1:1-5 is saying what happened on the first day of Creation. "In the beginning God created the heaven and the earth. And the earth was without form, and void; and darkness was upon the face of the deep. And the Spirit of God moved upon the face of the waters. And God said, Let there be light: and there was light. And God saw the light, that it was good: and God divided the light from the darkness. And God called the light Day, and the darkness he called Night. And the evening and the morning were the first day." (Genesis 1:1-5).

C.I. Scofield in his cross reference and notes state, "Earth made waste and empty by judgment." (Jeremiah 4:23-26) he inserted this for the "gap" between Genesis 1:1 and 1:2.

He must not of realize that there is a "and" that connects Genesis 1:1 and 1:2. The definition for the word "and" from the Webster's Dictionary is as follows: including, plus together with, in addition to, also. "And" is used as a conjunction which means, act of joining sentences together. Actually the word "and" is used 97 times in the 31 verses of Genesis chapter 1.

All 31 verses in Genesis chapter 1 is giving us what took place on the six days of Creation.

In Exodus chapter 20 verse 11 the Scripture states, "For in six days the LORD made the heaven and earth, the sea, and all that in them is, and rested the seventh day: wherefore the LORD blessed the sabbath day, and hallowed it."

The Scripture clearly states it took six days from "In the beginning" to create the heaven, earth, the sea, and all the other things God created in that time span. It was in 6 literal 24 hour days that God did this. Because at the end of each day the Lord said it was "the evening and morning" of that particular day (first through sixth). How foolish to believe that each "day" in Genesis chapter 1 stands for a particular geological era according to Hugh Miller and his "DAY-AGE THEORY". God said after the sixth day of Creation that what He created was "very good". "And God saw every thing that he had made, and, behold, it was very good. and the evening and the morning were the sixth day." (Genesis 1:31)

In Genesis 2:1-2 God said that took Him six days to complete Creation. "Thus the heavens and the earth were finished, and all the host of them. And on the seventh day God ended his work which he had made; and he rested on the seventh day from all his work which he had made." I see from God's Word (King James Authorized Version) that God only took six days from Genesis 1:1 to 1:31 to complete His work of Creation.

## 2. THE GAP THEORY IS UNSCRIPTURAL

No where in the Word of God does our Lord and Saviour Jesus Christ mention anything about a "gap" between when He made (created) the Heaven (outerspace) and the Earth of Genesis 1:1. Then by God's judgment decided to destroy the Earth by water because of Lucifer's sin in Genesis 1:2.

People who believe the Gap Theory is true try to use the following Scriptures to support it: (II PETER 3:5-7), (Jeremiah 4:23-26), (isaiah 24:1), (Isaiah 45:18).

*II PETER 3:5-7:* "For this they willingly are ignorant of, that by the word of God the heavens were of old, and the earth standing out of the water and in the water: Whereby the world that then was, being overflowed with water perished: But the heavens and the earth, which are now, by the same word are kept in store, reserved unto fire against the day of judgment and perdition of ungodly men."

This portion of Scripture is not talking about a flood that happened between Genesis 1:1 and Genesis 1:2. But is talking about the Noahaic Flood that occurred in Genesis chapters 7 and 8. In II peter 2:5, Peter is clearly telling us what flood he is talking about in II Peter 3:6.

"And spared not the old world, but saved Noah the eighth person, a preacher of righteousness, bringing in the flood upon the world of the ungodly." (II Peter 2:5).

Even C.I. Scofield in his cross reference is using Scriptures that are saying that II Peter 3:6 is the Noahiac Flood. Here is the following Scriptures he uses: (Genesis 7:26-27), (Matthew 24:37-39), (Luke 17:26-27) (II Peter 2:5). Even though Scofield believed in the Noahaic Flood. He still believed in the "GAP THEORY" and uses the next Scriptures to support it.

*JEREMIAH 4:23-26*: "I beheld the earth, and, lo, it was without form, and void; and the heavens, and they had no light. I beheld the mountains, and, lo, they trembled, and all the hills moved lightly. I beheld, and, lo, there was no man, and all the birds of the heavens were fled. I beheld, and, lo, the fruitful place was a wilderness, and all the cities thereof were broken down at the presence of the LORD, and by his fierce anger."

This is another portion of Scripture that the GAP THEORISTS use to support their theory between Genesis 1:1 and Genesis 1:2.

C.I. Scofield uses these verses in his cross reference and footnotes as a reference to the GAP THEORY. He says that Jeremiah 4:23 cross references to Genesis 1:2. His footnote states: (4:23) cf. Gen. 1:2 "Without form and void" describes the condition of the earth as the result of the judgment (vs. 24-26; Isa. 24:1) which overthrew the primal order of Gen. 1:1.

Jeremiah 4:23-26 is talking about a prophetic future event. This prophetic future event is about the nation of Israel. Jeremiah was praying to God about Israel and the city of Jerusalem. This future event is describing the Great Tribulation Period that will try the the whole earth that are left behind after the Rapture (Translation of the Church) has taking place. Israel will flee to the wilderness to escape the Antichrist (Jeremiah 4:26-31), (Revelation 12:5-6, 13-14).

*ISAIAH 24:1*: "Behold, the LORD maketh the earth empty, and maketh it waste, and turneth it upside down, and scattereth abroad the inhabitants thereof."

C.I. Scofield is saying in his cross reference that this portion of Scripture is in reference to Genesis 1:2.

This portion of Scripture is not talking about no such past event, but about a future event. This future prophetic event is the Great Tribulation Period that will literally rock this earth (Isaiah 24:20), (Revelation 6:12-17). Isaiah 24:6 is a key verse to verse 1. "Therefore hath the curse devoured the earth, and they that dwell therein are desolate: therefore the inhabitants of the earth are burned, and few men left." I do not see a flood of water here. I see fire ("inhabitants of the earth are burned" correlates with Revelation 16:8-9) and see that there is inhabitants left after this fire ("few men left").

Isaiah 24:1-23 is talking about the Great Tribulation Period and about the Battle of Armageddon after which the Lord Jesus Christ will reign from Jerusalem.

*ISAIAH 45:18*: "For thus saith the LORD that created the heavens; God himself that formed the earth and made it; he hath established it, he created it not in vain, he formed it to be inhabited: I am the LORD; and there is none else."

C.I. Scofield says this portion of Scripture clearly indicates that the earth had undergone a cataclysmic change as a result of a divine judgment.

I do not see that here. I see the creation of the universe and the earth. This portion of Scripture clearly tells us of the creative processes that God did to the Earth to make it inhabitable for living creatures. Because God said that He created the Earth not in vain. Which means that the Earth He created was "very good" and He sums this up in Genesis 1:31. "And God saw every thing that he made, and behold, it was very good. And the evening and the morning were the sixth day."

To say the Earth that God created was destroyed by Lucifer's flood (judgment) would say that God created the Earth "In the beginning" in vain. That would be calling God a liar. Because God said in Isaiah 45:18 that He did not create the Earth in vain: "God himself that formed the earth and made it; he hath established it, he created it not in vain," It says in Scripture that it is impossible (cannot) for God to lie (Hebrews 6:18), (Titus 1:2). It is man who lies using his man-made doctrine, philosophies, and theories not God (Colossians 2:8).

1. To believe in the "GAP THEORY" man tries to harmonize Genesis 1:1 and Genesis 1:2 with the popular belief that geologists provide "undeniable evidence" that the world is exceedingly old (billions of years). This is nothing more than theistic evolution. The "GAP THEORY" is a man-made doctrine.
2. It is time for those who are Bible-Believers (King James Authorized Version) to abandon the "GAP THEORY" or any other theory that is God-dishonoring and simple believe what God has said. Because the "GAP THEORY" has no biblical merit. There is no Scripture that supports it.
3. The Evolution lie is taking hold. The "GAP THEORY" rides on the back of the Evolution lie giving credence to it.
4. We as Born-Again Bible-Believing Christians must give glory to God for what He has said in the Book of Genesis. And believe what He created ("In the beginning") was very good and not tainted with sin until Adam's fall in the Garden of Eden. Romans 5:12-14 says, "Wherefore, as by one man sin entered into the world, and death by sin; and so death passed upon all men, for that all have sinned: (For until the law sin was in the world: but sin is not imputed when there is no law. Nevertheless death reigned from Adam to Moses, even over them that had not sinned after the similitude of Adam's transgression, who is the figure of him that was to come."

But we have a Saviour who took away this sin once and for all the Lord Jesus Christ (Romans 5:8-11), (Hebrews 10:9-11).

# Conclusion

MANY OF THE creatures listed in this book lived on this Earth at one time or another. We know this by the fossil skeletons that have been unearthed by men who believed that they existed but did not have proof until they discovered them. It was by faith that these men and women dedicated their time and effort searching and digging until they found what they believe existed. This is the same belief that drives people to look for the hidden animals that are so elusive to man.

Many cultures have in their folklore, legends, and mythology of creatures so fantastic that other cultures ridiculed them for believing in such a notion. People who believe in Cryptozoology also get the same from mainstream scientists. So to believe in Biblical Cryptozoology would be a double whammy. Not so because every thing that has been revealed in the Bible has been seen by men who were real people who have written down their eyewitness accounts. I believe it not only takes faith but saving faith to believe this. God will give you this saving faith when you receive His Son as personal Lord and Saviour. You will get a peace that passes all understanding. "Therefore being justified by faith, we have peace with God through our Lord Jesus Christ"-Romans 5:1.

Another thing needed to be a Biblical Cryptozoologist is to hone your observation skills. Four simple rules to follow when you are investigating is: 1. Document everything 2. Examine everything you can time premitting 3. Support your evidence 4. Record all testimony.

Tools needed are your Bible, prayer, Biblical Cryptozoology Report, pen or pencil, tablet or notebook, flashlight, and a good sturdy day-pack to carry everything in. Yes, also do not forget your camera if you have one. Preferably one that uses film so you have a negative to back your investigation. Negatives can be analyze easily.

# BIBLICAL CRYTOZOOLOGY REPORT

DATE:

## GENERAL INFORMATION

Type of Sighting: _____ Date of Occurrence _____

Location of Sighting: _____

Type of Cryptid:
_____

Has creature been seen before by same parties? ☐ Yes ☐ No If Yes, please list: _____
_____
_____
_____

Physical Address (where sighting occurred – *no* P.O. boxes):
_____

City: _____ State: _____ ZIP: _____ How Long? ___ yrs ___ mos.

Main Phone: ( ) _____ Fax: ( ) _____ Is this a residential? ☐ Yes ☐ No

Other location information: _____
_____

Did sightings occur indoors at this location? (please check one)   ☐ Outdoors ☐ Indoors

## WITNESS INFORMATION
### USE EXTRA SHEETS IF NECESSARY

Total Number of Witnesses _____

Witness 1: _____

Occupation: _____ Phone: ( ) _____

Primary Email: _____ Secondary Email: _____

Gender: _____ Birth Information: _____

Residential Street Address: _____

City: _____ State: _____ ZIP: _____

Witness 2: _____

Occupation: _____ Phone: ( ) _____

Primary Email: _____ Secondary Email: _____

Gender: _____ Birth Information: _____

Residential Street Address: _____

City: _____ State: _____ ZIP: _____

## PHYSICAL EVIDENCE COLLECTED

List all physical evidence at scene (including photographs): _____

## DESCRIPTION OF SIGHTINGS
### USE EXTRA SHEETS IF NECESSARY

Print Name of Investigator       Email address or Telephone

X
Investigator's Authorized Signature        Date

# Glossary of Terms

Abominable Snowman: Also known as Yeti, a hairy apelike creature who inhabits the Himalayan mountains.

Basilosaurus: A elongated sea creature that swam in a serpentine motion that grew to 60 feet or more. Also called a Zueglodon from the valley in Egypt were fossils of it were found.

Beasts: Animals mentioned in the Bible. They are brutal towards man. synonyms of beast are monster, savage, brute, creature, and animal.

Behemoth: Colossal creature with a tail that moved like a mighty cedar that is described in the Book of Job.

Biblical: Things pretaining to the Word of God (Bible).

Bigfoot: A tall, hairy ape-like creature that got its name from a plaster cast of a large footprint in the Bluff Creek Valley in 1958.

Blue Whale: Is a marine mammal that can reach the length of 100 feet.

Cadborosaurus: A serpent reported to be living on the Pacific coast of North America. Its name is derived from Cadboro Bay in Victoria, British Columbia. Its nickname is "Caddy".

Champ: Name given to the lake monster living in Lake Champlain. The 1977 photograph that Sandra Mansi took of the creature has been the best known photo of the creature.

Coelacanth: A member of the lobe-finned fishes called Crossopterygians that were thought to be extinct until rediscovered in 1938 off the coast of South Africa.

Creation: All things that were created by God in 6 solar (24-hour) days.

Cryptid: Are creatures presumed extinct, hypothetical species, or creatures known from anecedotal evidence or evidence insufficient to prove their existence.

Cryptozoology: Is the study of hidden animals that are elusive to man. Their reported existence is unproven.

Dinosaurs: Creatures presumed extinct. A Greek word meaning "Terrible Lizards". Many Fossil skeletons have been unearth of these creatures.

Diplodocus: Is a member of the group of dinosaurs called Sauropods. They had long necks and long tails and were herbivores (plant eaters). The first complete fossil skeleton of one was unearthed in 1899. It is displayed at the Carnegie Museum of Natural History in Pittsburgh, Pennsylvania.

Dragons: Mythical creatures in folklore that were thought to breath fire and could fly. Actually they are real creatures described in the Bible.

| | |
|---|---|
| Elasmosaurus: | It was longest of the plesiosaurs. It had a long neck, large body and four flippers. Many people believe the Loch Ness Monster is this creature. |
| Emela-Ntouka: | Literally means killer of elephants. |
| Fiery Flying Serpent: | Creature described in the Bible as being red in color and had wings for flying. Description fits the group of flying reptiles called Pterosaurs. |
| Jersey Devil: | Creature described as being the size of a crane with a long neck, long back legs with cloven hooves, short front legs with paws and bat-like wings, and a head of a horse or dog. |
| Komodo Dragon: | Large monitor lizard that measure up to 10 feet and weigh up to 300 lbs. They live on the Komodo Islands of Indonesia. |
| Kongamato: | Flying reptile reported in Africa with smooth skin, a beak full of sharp teeth, and wings with bat-like skin, they are believed to be a type of pterosaur. |
| Kronosaurus: | One of the largest plisosaurs. It had a large skull over 10 feet, short neck, and stocky body. It had teeth that measured over 10 inches long. |
| Leviathan: | Large sea creatures that were also called sea serpents. They are described in the Bible as having large bodies, strong jaws and great teeth. |
| Loch Ness Monster: | Legendary creature claimed to inhabit Scotland's Loch Ness. Given the nickname "Nessie". |
| Megalania: | An extinct giant monitor over 23 feet long. |
| Mokele-Mbembe: | Described by Congo pygmies as half elephant and half dragon that looks like a sauropod dinosaur. |
| Ogopogo: | Giant serpentine creature known to inhabit Lake Okanagan in British Columbia, Canada. |

Rhamphorhynchus: A long-tailed pterosaur. It was only about 7 inches long with a 3 foot wingspan. Its name means "beak jaw".

Satyrs: In Greek mythology they were creatures of the forest and mountains. They are described in the Bible as being hairy ones.

Sauropods: Presumed extinct long necked dinosaurs in which the Diplodocus is a member of.

Styracosaurus: A dinosaur belonging to the group called Ceratopsians (horned-ones). It had a single horn and looked like a rhinoceros.

Tanystropheus: A bizarre looking reptile with a neck longer than its body and tail combined. When first discovered in 1886 it was mistaken for a pterosaur (flying reptile). The neck bones were mistaken for wing bones. This was not corrected until 1929.

Tsintaosaurus: A duck-billed dinosaur with a single horn on its head.

Unicorn: A creature that has a single horn on its head. As described in the Bible it also has great strength.

Yeti: See Abominable Snowman

Zeuglodon: See Basilosaurus

# References

"A Fighting Chance" pages 12, 131-132 John Ridgeway & Chay Blyth

"Alien Animals" pages 170-171, Janet and colin Bord

"A Living Dinosaur" page 247, 1987, Roy Mackal

"Dinosaurs by Design" 1992, Duane Gish

"Dinosaurs & other Prehistoric Animals" page 9, 1959, Darlene Geis

"Holy Bible" (King James Version)

"In the Wake of Sea-Serpents" pages 198-217, Bernard Huevelmans

"In Witchbound Africa" Frank H. Melland

"Living Dinosaur" 1987, Roy Mackal

"Mermaids and Mastodons" pages 23-24, Richard Carrington

"On the Track of Unknown Animals" 1959, Bernard Huevelmans

"The Mothman Prophecies" John A. Keel

"The Wikipedia free encyclopedia"

"The New York Times" October 18 & December 10, 1981

---

*Four Things You Should Know!*

1. YOU NEED TO BE SAVED ..................................................Romans 3:23
   *"For all have sinned, and come short of the glory of God;"*
2. YOU CANNOT SAVE YOURSELF ................................Romans 6:23
   *"For the wages of sin is death; but the gift of God is eternal life through Jesus Christ our Lord."*
3. JESUS CAN SAVE YOU ......................................................John 3:16
   *"For God so loved the world, that he gave his only begotten Son, that whosoever believeth in him should not perish, but have everlasting life."*
4. BE SAVED NOW ....................................................................Romans 10:13
   *"For whosoever shall call upon the name of the Lord shall be saved."*

---

*My Decision to Receive Christ as My Saviour*

Confession to God that I am a sinner, and believing that the Lord Jesus Christ died for my sins on the cross and was raised for my justification, I do now receive and confess Him as my personal Saviour.

_____
NAME

_____
DATE

*Assurance as a Believer*

"That if thou shalt confess with thy mouth the Lord Jesus, and shalt believe in thine heart that God hath raised Him from the dead, thou shalt be saved. For with the heart man believeth unto righteousness; and with the mouth confession is made unto salvation."

– *Romans 10:9-10*

# AMEN

"... These things saith the Amen, the faithful and true witness, the beginning of the creation of God;" (Revelation 3:14)

*"The Lord Jesus Christ is the Amen."*

Alleluia –

"And after these things I heard a great voice of much people in heaven, saying, Alleluia; Salvation, and glory, and honour, and power, unto the Lord our God:" (Revelation 19:1)

"And I heard as it were the voice of a great multitude, and as the voice of many waters, and as the voice of mighty thunderings, saying, Alleluia: for the Lord God omnipotent reigneth." (Revelation 19:6)

Magnify –

"O magnify the LORD with me, and let us exalt his name together." (Psalm 34:3)

"Let all those that seek thee rejoice and be glad in thee: let such as love thy salvation say continually, The LORD be magnified." (Psalm 40:16)

Exalt –

"Exalt ye the LORD our God, worship at his footstool; for he is holy." (Psalm 99:5)

"Thou art my God, and I will praise thee: thou art my God, I will exalt thee." (Psalm 118:28)

Name –

"O LORD our Lord, how excellent is thy name in all the earth! who hast set thy glory above the heavens." (Psalm 8:1)

"I will praise the LORD according to his righteousness: and will sing praise to the name of the LORD most high." (Psalm 7:17)

"Give unto the LORD the glory due unto his name; worship the LORD in the beauty of holiness." (Psalm 29:2)

"I will praise thee, O LORD my God, with all my heart: and I will glorify thy name for evermore." (Psalm 86:12)

"For all the promises of God in him are yea, and in him Amen, unto the glory of God by us." (II Corinthians 1:20)

Made in the USA
Lexington, KY
18 August 2012